Joseph Stalin

From Peasant to Premier

Joseph Stalin

From Peasant to Premier

Nancy Whitelaw

A People in Focus Book

DILLON PRESS
New York

1992

Maxwell Macmillan Canada
Toronto
Maxwell Macmillan International
New York Oxford Singapore Sydney

To the Write People, with thanks and love

Photo Credits

Cover image: AP—Wide World Photos
Back image: AP—Wide World Photos

The Bettmann Archive: 11, 13, 20, 38, 69, 75, 77, 84, 100, 119, 128
Sovfoto: 14, 30
Library of Congress: 34
AP—Wide World Photos: 45, 59, 87, 90, 107, 110, 136, 137

Library of Congress Cataloging-in-Publication Data

Whitelaw, Nancy.
    Joseph Stalin: from peasant to premier/by Nancy Whitelaw. —1st ed.
        p.   cm — (People in focus series)
    Includes bibliographical references.
    Summary: Examines the life and times of Joseph Stalin, the dictatorial
leader of the Soviet Union from 1925 to 1953.
        ISBN 0-87518-557-6
        1. Stalin, Joseph, 1879-1953—Juvenile literature. 2. Soviet Union—
History—1925-1953—Juvenile literature. [1. Stalin, Joseph, 1879-1953. 2.
Heads of state. 3. Soviet Union—History—1925-1953.] I. Title.
II. Series.
DK268.S3W47   1992
947.084'2'092—dc20
[B]
                                                                            92-5747

Dillon Press   Maxwell Macmillan Canada, Inc.
Macmillan Publishing Company   1200 Eglinton Avenue East
866 Third Avenue   Suite 200
New York, NY 10022   Don Mills, Ontario M3C 3N1

Macmillan Publishing Company is part of the Maxwell Communication Group
of Companies.

First edition
Printed in the United States of America
10 9 8 7 6 5 4 3 2 1

Acknowledgments

The author is grateful to Mark von Hagen, associate professor of history, Columbia University, who read the manuscript and offered many valuable suggestions. She would also like to thank Joyce Stanton for her competent and good-humored editing.

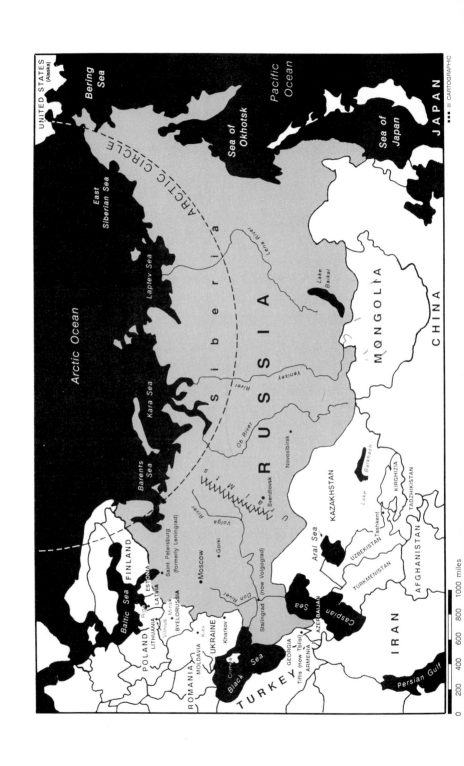

III CARTOGRAPHIC

0   200   400   600   800   1000 miles

Contents

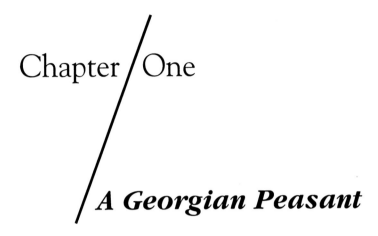

Chapter / One

A Georgian Peasant

On the night of October 31, 1961, Soviet soldiers raised the lid of a glass-covered coffin and took out the stiff body of Generalissimo Joseph Stalin. They carried it up the stairs and out into Red Square. There police were waiting to transfer the remains to a new grave.

Although the sky was dark, this corner of Moscow was bright with floodlights. They shone on the jeeps, troop carriers, and armored cars that guarded the area. They lighted up the enormous black-and-red mausoleum, the building that had housed Stalin's body. They twinkled on the medals of his uniform.

The police carried their burden to a small cemetery behind the magnificent mausoleum.

There they dug a hole, placed the body inside, and covered it with dirt. They placed a small, flat gravestone on the newly shoveled earth. Someone added a vase of 12 white chrysanthemums.

This event was reported in *Newsweek* in November 1961. There are people who say it is not true. That is the way it is with stories about Joseph Stalin, the man who ruled the Soviet Union for nearly 30 years. For every story—and there are plenty—there are people who tell a different version.

Histories of Stalin's life hold more questions than answers. During his lifetime, some called him the hope of the world's poor and the greatest of all leaders. Others called him the most cruel and evil man who ever lived.

The whole story of his life is not yet known. Hundreds of historians have become detectives as they search the records to find answers. Some of what they read and hear is true. Some of what they find is totally false or partly false, exaggerated or not complete. Thus, it is not possible to know for certain which details of his life are true.

We do know that the man known as Stalin was christened Iosif Vissarionovich Dzhugashvili in

1879. He was born in Georgia, one of many nations loosely connected to the Russian Empire. Georgians were subjects of the czar, as were the people of the other nations, including Russia, Ukraine, Byelorussia, Armenia, and parts of Siberia. Because the czar came from Russia and because Russia was the most populous nation, the empire was known as the Russian Empire.

Stalin's parents were peasants who did not always have enough money to buy staples such as bread and tea. Poverty was a way of life for the Dzhugashvilis and millions of other peasants, just as it had been for their parents, grandparents, great-grandparents—as far back as families could remember.

Not all subjects of the czar were poor. Some nobles and lords lived in marble palaces, and they did not seem to see the peasants' flimsy shacks. They wore ermine and mink, and maybe they did not know how the Russian cold bit through thin jackets and felt boots. They ate French pastries and blini—pancakes heaped with caviar—and they drank wine from golden goblets. Some factory workers' children starved to death on city streets near the palaces of the nobles.

Like nine out of every ten subjects, Joseph Dzhugashvili's father was born a serf, a peasant who was under the total control of a lord. A serf was assigned a plot of land, which he plowed, planted, and harvested. Then he handed over a portion of the produce to the landowner. He was not allowed to move off the land and become independent. In fact, he had no rights at all.

From time to time, the serfs in the Russian Empire tried to improve their lot. They demonstrated in city squares, they marched to the palaces of the rulers, they called on landowners. Sometimes they asked for bread, sometimes for better working conditions, sometimes for the right to own land.

The answer from the nobles was always no, and the serfs answered back by demonstrating more often and more loudly. Finally Czar Alexander II feared that he could no longer control the demonstrations. In 1861 he issued the Emancipation Edict, abolishing serfdom.

Freeing the serfs in the Russian Empire was something like freeing the slaves in the United States. The freed persons celebrated, but only for a very short time. After a few weeks of triumph, the

The village of Gori, where Stalin grew up

serfs, like the slaves, discovered that they were not able to earn a living. They had no money, no land, and few skills. Many went back to their former lords to work for a bare existence.

Joseph's father was one who did not want to go back to the farm. Instead he became a cobbler in Gori, a village in Georgia. Situated between the Black Sea and the Caspian Sea, Georgia was bright with flowers and rich with orchards. But the life of the Dzhugashvili family was neither bright nor rich.

Joseph's first home was a drab wooden building at 10 Sobornya Street. He and his parents lived in two rooms. In sunny weather, two small windows caught some of the bright rays. In rainy weather, the family put wooden bowls on the brick floor to catch drips from the leaky roof. The furnishings consisted of a stove, a small table, wooden stools, and a plank bed with a straw mattress.

But according to many historians, the worst part of young Joseph's homelife was not the poverty; it was his father, Vissarion, who often acted like a madman. He was a stout man with heavy black eyebrows and a thick black mustache. It has been said that he enjoyed beating both his son and his wife, and that he stopped only when their faces and bodies were covered with bruises, or when he was tired.

Vissarion Dzhugashvili was not unusual, however, in his brutality. The Russian peasants—hardened by hundreds of years of oppression, ignorance, and superstition—often knew no other way but brutality to vent their frustrations.

As her husband drank more and worked less, Joseph's mother, Ekaterina, struggled to help support the family by cleaning, laundering, baking bread, sewing, and running errands.

When Joseph was four years old, Vissarion left the family home to work in a shoe factory in Tiflis (called Tbilisi today), about a hundred miles away. Joseph's mother then had to support herself and her son alone.

Young Joseph—pictured in the bottom right corner—with some schoolmates

Ekaterina, Joseph's devoted mother

Ekaterina Dzhugashvili had married when she was an 18-year-old red-haired beauty. She lost three children in childbirth. Joseph was the only child who lived. It has been said that as much as Vissarion hated Joseph, that was how much Ekaterina loved the little boy.

Ekaterina brought happiness to young Joseph. She sang for him, teaching him centuries-old Georgian folk songs. On holidays and feast days, she put aside her shapeless faded dresses and simple kerchiefs. Instead she wore rainbow-colored skirts and long, floating veils. And whenever she could, she kept her child's stomach full, serving him good roast meat, red beans, boiled potatoes, and fruit.

Ekaterina had two joys in her life—her son, whom she nicknamed Soso, and the church. When Joseph was an infant, she would rock him and whisper, "My Soso, my son, someday you will be a fine priest."

Both little Joseph and his mother loved the Orthodox church. Inside the sacred building, they were surrounded by holy paintings called icons, colored in reds, greens, and golds. Flickering candles cast mysterious shadows on the arched ceiling, and smoky perfume filled the air as deacons swung the gold censers.

The bishop began the service by putting on his bright green-and-gold robes, and adjusting several crucifixes and crosses on his chest. Finally he set the heavy jeweled crown on his head.

Then came the readings of the Gospels, a special treat for the peasants, who could not read themselves. Perhaps Joseph loved best the story of Saint Joseph, for whom he was named. The singing of the all-male choir, the majesty of the robes and icons, the beauty of the rituals—these helped the congregation to forget their empty stomachs and their cold feet as they stood on the stone floor of the church for ceremonies that lasted three and four hours at a time.

Joseph became part of the beauty, wearing colorful vestments, walking in processions, and—best of all to him—singing. How he loved the hymns and the chants!

Religion was a part of his life at the local school, too. No wonder he thought about becoming a priest. His first schoolbook was the Book of Psalms. The Orthodox church in the Russian Empire was closely connected to the government and the schools. Nobles granted funds to the church, and they encouraged people to become church members. In return, the church officials urged the congregation to be faithful to the czar and his rule. Religious school lessons included:

Question: Whom shall we honor?
Answer: First, and most of all, the czar.
Question: How should we show respect to
              the czar?
Answer: We should be prepared to lay
              down our lives for him.

Joseph also studied the Russian language, ancient Greek, Hebrew, arithmetic, drawing, science, and music. His student uniform was a jacket with a stand-up collar, and baggy brown trousers. He was neither handsome nor homely, a rather ordinary-looking student except that his face was scarred from the smallpox that he had contracted when he was seven years old. Also, his left arm was permanently stiff because of a childhood accident.

Some say Joseph was a dreamer, a young boy who lived more often in the legends of the past than in the present. He loved these tales, which had been handed down through generations of

Georgians. He cared more for reading than for making friends, said Joseph Iremashvili, one of his few friends.

One of Joseph's heroes in the legends was Koba. This character was loyal to his friends and ruthless toward his enemies. Joseph told Iremashvili that in his deepest thoughts he became Koba, the fierce hero who always sought revenge against those he felt had wronged him.

In later years, Iremashvili recalled his adventures with Joseph. The summers in Georgia were comfortably cool, and the boys played outside near the flourishing peach and pear orchards, fields of golden wheat, and thick-leaved vineyards. They explored the crumbling fortress on the hill, swam in the slow-flowing Kura River, and played a game called war against Russia, which was similar to cops and robbers. In the fall, they wrestled in the crisp golden leaves of oak and cherry-laurel trees.

When he was ten, Joseph's father forced him to go to Tiflis to work in the shoe factory with him. Before many months had passed, Joseph's mother came to take him back to Gori. She insisted that her son become a priest, not a cobbler.

Joseph saw little of his father after that. The man died when his son was 11 years old.

After his graduation from the local grammar school, when he was about 14, Joseph and his mother agreed that he would train to be a priest of the Orthodox church they loved so much. Joseph was given a scholarship to the all-male Tiflis Theological Seminary. The scholarship paid for uniforms, shoes, board and room, and textbooks. He was 15 years old in 1894 when he left home to go to the school.

No one knows why Joseph wanted to enter the seminary. Did he want to become a man of peace because he had grown up with the hatred and brutality of his father? Was he in love with the beauty of the ceremonies and the church buildings? Or did he see the seminary, the only college in Georgia, merely as a place in which he could further his education?

In any case, he knew that many seminary students did not become priests. In fact, many graduates became leaders in radical and revolutionary movements.

Joseph may have been depressed when he first

Joseph at the Tiflis Theological Seminary, age 15

saw the bars on the windows of the dark and gloomy seminary building. His schedule was even more depressing. His courses included the prayers and chants of the church, Russian composition, the Bible, and Slavonic, an ancient church language.

Students were awakened at 7:00 A.M. to attend services for a couple of hours in the chapel. After a light breakfast, they studied, then prayed, and then studied again. After a light lunch, they studied and then prayed again. Between 3:00 and 5:00, they were allowed to go on supervised walks around the city. After dinner came more prayers and more studying. On Sundays the students stood on the stone floors of the church for hours during the services.

It is not surprising that many of the young men protested. When they did, the priests scolded and threatened to expel them.

Joseph broke one rule 14 times. It was the banned-book rule. School officials issued a long list of books that were forbidden to students. These included books describing the lives of poor people in Russia, some sophisticated European romances, and certain foreign books such as *On the Origin of Species* by the English scientist Charles Darwin.

Joseph borrowed these books from a lending library in town. The priests caught him, scolded him, and put in him solitary confinement. After his punishment, he returned to the library as soon as he could for more forbidden books.

He also wrote poetry, and historians pore over his verses now, trying to find clues to his personality development.

Chapter / Two

From Student to Revolutionary

Most of Joseph's poetry was about his love for his country. One of his poems, "To the Moon," shows how he was beginning to think about working for changes in Georgia.

> *Know well that those who once*
> *Fell to the oppressors*
> *Shall rise again and soar,*
> *Winged with bright hope,*
> *Above the sacred mountain.*

"Those who once fell to the oppressors" were the pitifully poor Georgian farmers and workers. Was Joseph thinking that he would lead his people to rise up against their oppressors?

How could anyone rise against Czar Nicholas II,

who had complete power over the empire? He seemed to be unconcerned about the suffering of his people. Nicholas II spent a lot of time with his wife and children, and he loved balls and parties.

Three classes of people lived in the empire. At the top, a small group of nobles owned most of the land and wealth. Next there was a small middle class of professional people—doctors, teachers, and lawyers. Then there was a huge group of peasants and factory workers. Like Joseph's father, they were unskilled, uneducated, and wretchedly poor.

Factory workers led desperate lives. Six days a week, they worked 13 or 14 hours a day, and they barely made enough money to keep from starving.

In western Europe, factory workers were beginning to fight against such conditions. Intellectuals and students urged the workers to join them in the Socialist party, a group that believed in an economic system where wealth would be shared by all citizens. These Socialists dreamed that workers from all over Europe and the Russian Empire would rise up at the same time in a massive revolution. They traveled to Russia to extend socialism there.

Although seminary students were forbidden to join the Socialist party, Joseph and many of his friends were excited by the ideas: Overthrow the czar! Create a new government! Demonstrate! Strike!

In 1899 Joseph officially became a Socialist. Many nights the 20-year-old student climbed out of windows and slid down outside walls to attend meetings. As he listened to the leaders talk, he began to think about becoming a leader himself.

The stories he heard were exciting. The speakers were forceful. Revolution was in the air. Over and over again, he heard stories of government brutality against workers. These acts included whipping, torture, and murder. The Socialists urged working people from all over Georgia, from all over the empire, from all over the world, to fight against tyrants.

Joseph became more involved in the revolutionary movement and less interested in school. Iremashvili wrote later that Joseph became short-tempered with other students and with the teachers. He expected everyone to agree with him, and he became enraged when they did not.

Ambition grew fast in the young man. He spent hours in the railroad yards, trying to convince the workers there to stage strikes, to sabotage trains and damage tracks, to create problems for the railroad and the government.

At this point—the beginning of his fifth year at the seminary—he hardly attended classes at all. When he was reprimanded by the priests, he either refused to talk or gave a rude answer. Perhaps the memory of his father's cruel discipline caused him to rebel against the priests' authority.

So Joseph left school. The seminary record states:

> May 29, 1899. Iosif Dzhugashvili is dismissed from the Seminary for having missed his examinations for an unexplained reason.

In 1931 Stalin wrote in his autobiography, *Works XIII:*

> In protest against . . . the seminary, I became a revolutionary. . . . [The priests'] method is spying, prying, worming their way into people's souls. . . . What good can there be in that? . . . The bell rings for morning tea, we go to the dining room, and when we return to our rooms we find that a search has been made and all our chests have been ransacked.

It seems clear that he left with an even deeper hatred of authority than he had felt when he had entered the school.

There he was, 20 years old, with no diploma and without definite plans for the future. Only two things were sure—he did not want to be a priest, and he was not afraid to rebel.

He talked with young men who dreamed about a world in which all men would be truly equal. Their guide was a book by Karl Marx, *The Communist Manifesto*. Marx believed that greed was the root of evil. He advocated an economic system in which the government would control major sources of production and guarantee adequate food, clothing, and shelter for all citizens. Marx's theory of communism would do away with capitalism, where private individuals and corporations control production.

Marx stated that economic and political changes would occur only through violent revolution. Researchers have wondered whether the violence of the proposed movement was more appealing to Joseph than its economic ideals.

Joseph had to make a living, so he got a job as a clerk at an observatory at Tiflis in December

1899. He spent all his spare time with party members, scheming against the government, passing out crudely printed pamphlets to railroad and factory workers, and speaking to anyone who would listen to him talk about the need to overthrow the government.

Joseph wore a black shirt and red scarf like other revolutionaries, but he did not look or sound like a powerful leader. He was only five feet four inches tall. He spoke in a harsh voice, and he had the accent of an uncultured provincial. Still, his audiences listened. Perhaps the older ones wanted to believe that they could be free, and the younger ones wanted to believe that they could be powerful. Many could not read or write, and they admired Joseph for his seminary education.

A revolutionary cycle began. Members of workers' organizations became bolder, and the police became bolder about arresting them. The workers reacted by becoming more angry and even more bold.

In April 1901, 2,000 people gathered in the center of Tiflis to demonstrate. Police attacked with swords and whips, injuring 14 of them and arresting 50. Joseph wrote that this demonstration had been a great success. When some revolutionaries are hurt, he said, the rest will double their anger. He believed it was through such anger and hatred that the revolution would succeed. "Women and children must be hurt, too. . . . The whiplash is rendering us a great service, for it is hastening the revolution."

Joseph wrote articles for an underground newspaper, capturing readers' imaginations with a style he had developed from the chants in the seminary.

> . . . groaning is the hunger-swollen Russian peasantry. . . .
> Groaning are the small town-dwellers. . . .
> Groaning too is the lower and even middle class . . .

Apparently the police heard that Joseph kept piles of forbidden literature, because one day they stormed into his room.

They found nothing. Not even Joseph.

They dashed over to his mother's home. He was not there, either.

Where was he? For months he had been moving from one friend's home to another, always a step ahead of the police. Where was the forbidden literature? He had hidden it under a pile of bricks on the bank of the nearby Kura River.

After about two years, Joseph quit the Tiflis organization. Or was he thrown out? No one is sure. Disagreement arose over the appointment of workers to important positions in the party. Joseph argued that only intellectuals like himself were qualified to lead.

In late 1901, Joseph arrived in Batumi, a city on the Black Sea, ready to unite the city's 30,000 workers. For five months, he cranked out pamphlets, headed "study circles"—he told police they were social parties—and urged street demonstrations.

Demonstrations became routine. First came lines and lines of workers singing and waving red banners. Then came the mounted police to slash, shoot, run down, and make arrests. The demonstrators would run away.

The next day, the demonstrators would again form lines, and they would march and sing. The police would again attack with horses, swords, and guns. Day after day, the demonstrations continued.

Joseph learned to avoid the police. He frequently changed his name and address. Finally he took the name of Koba, his childhood hero, and this name remained with him for several years.

At one of the demonstrations, Koba met a

Demonstrations against the czar became routine as revolutionary activity grew.

small, pretty young woman with deep-set dark eyes. Ekaterina Svanidze was also a member of the revolutionary movement, and she and Koba became close friends.

But the police were on his trail. Koba was forced to become more careful. He moved into a nearby village and hid in the home of his friend Khashim Smirba.

The people of the village were curious when they saw a printing press go into the house. A few days later, Muslim women in long veils were seen entering the house. When these women left, they were carrying piles of paper. The villagers guessed that they were watching a counterfeit money operation.

Maybe they never found out that the "Muslim women" were disguised Socialist party members, and that the piles of "counterfeit money" were pamphlets urging revolutionary action against the czar.

Smirba hid some of the pamphlets on the bottoms of baskets of vegetables that he took to market for sale. Sometimes he wrapped the vegetables in the pamphlets.

The police trail grew closer, and Koba moved the printing press to the local cemetery.

The workers of Batumi were growing more angry and less cautious. During one strike, the police arrested a number of the leaders. The next day, all the workers in the city marched peacefully to the office of the military governor to protest the arrests. At the office, two workmen stepped out in front and asked that the arrested strikers be released. The officials and the workmen argued. Someone threw a rock, and the soldiers started shooting. When it was over, 14 workers were dead, 54 had been wounded, and more than 500 had been arrested.

A few days later, Koba was at a social gathering at a friend's house. A guest came in late and announced that the police had surrounded the house. A few minutes later, the police entered and arrested everyone.

Koba was caught. The police booked him. In the police photographs, he is a rather handsome young man with thick brown hair, a small and neat mustache, and a checkered red-and-white scarf. He was imprisoned on April 18, 1902.

Meanwhile, the Second Congress of the Russian Social Democratic Labour Party met in London because the party was outlawed in Russia. The party split into two factions, Bolsheviks and Mensheviks. Both parties advocated a revolutionary underground movement. The Bolsheviks supported Lenin as their leader. And the Mensheviks supported Yuli Martov.

Koba read about the meeting, and he chose Lenin as the man he wanted to follow.

For a year and a half after his arrest, Koba was confined in jail without a trial. Then in November 1903, he was sentenced to three years of exile in Nizhneudinsk, Siberia. This tiny village was a five-week trip from Batumi by train and dogsled! In much of Siberia, small villages were thousands of miles apart, and roads were little better than trails.

A police mug shot of "Koba" after his arrest

Siberia is a part of northern Russia that is as large as the 48 contiguous states of the United States. It is scarcely fit for human habitation. Winters are so cold that in some places the soil does not thaw all year. The town of Verkhoyansk has registered temperatures of –97°F (–72°C). In another town, small children are allowed to stay home from school when the temperature reaches –60°F (–51°C). And summer usually lasts for only a couple of months. This season is noted for temperatures as high as 100°F (38°C). Swarms of gnats and mosquitoes increase the discomfort.

In Siberia Koba was at least free to read, write, and study. He could also talk with other political prisoners. The only thing he could not do was leave the village.

Exile was not like jail. There was no prison building, no fences or walls, and just a few guards. The purpose of exile was to put convicted persons where they could not commit crimes or influence others to do so.

But life in exile was harsh. Some convicts were forced to toil on government projects. Food, clothing, and shelter were barely sufficient to keep prisoners alive. Few tried to escape, however. Escape meant going alone into frozen, hostile wilderness with no food or possible shelter.

Still Koba chose escape over imprisonment. This is the story he told: On Christmas Day, he stole a rifle from a drunken guard and started over the snow to the nearest village, 20 miles (32 kilometers) away. Before long a wolf threatened him. He shot the wolf. But other wolves heard the shot, and soon a pack began to close in on him. Darkness fell, and the temperature was far below zero. He was too tired to go on but was afraid to stop and rest. His only hope was to go back to his cabin, so he did.

A few days later, Koba walked away once

more. His story is that he found a sleigh driver who took him to a Socialist party sympathizer in Irkutsk. This sympathizer gave him a forged passport to use on a train heading south.

In February 1904, Koba was back in Tiflis. The political climate was at a boiling point. The country was losing an unpopular war with Japan. Subjects of the czar grew bolder in their protests. The czar's soldiers reacted with force and brutality.

Ekaterina Svanidze had remained faithful, and it was not long before she and Koba were married. Some historians say that Ekaterina begged him not to continue his secret activities, and that he did not listen to her.

Now an escaped convict, Koba was forced to keep moving from house to house to avoid being caught again. He wrote and distributed pamphlets, urging others to fight. "We must force the authorities to impose regressive measures," he wrote. "The worse they are, the better for us!"

Demonstrations! Marches! Beatings! The police response grew stronger.

Finally, on January 22, 1905, 200,000 workers gathered in Saint Petersburg, the capital of the empire. Led by a priest, they marched calmly to the czar's Winter Palace. They were coming to ask the czar, whom they called Little Father, to help them. They seemed to believe that the czar would make everything right if only he understood their suffering.

In front of the parade, they carried a huge picture of the czar and a large white flag that read SOLDIERS, DO NOT FIRE ON THE PEOPLE. Many carried religious banners, crosses, and icons. They brought a petition:

> Sire: We, workers and dwellers in Saint Petersburg, have come to thee, Sire, with our wives, daughters, and helpless old parents to seek truth and protection. . . .

By the time the procession reached the Winter Palace, the parade stretched back many blocks. Suddenly soldiers appeared from all sides, and shots rang out. The troopers shot the people as fast as they could reload their guns.

In a few hours, the bodies of marchers lay torn and bleeding on the white snow. Five hundred were dead and thousands were wounded.

The priest who had led the demonstration declared, "Peaceful means have failed. Now we must turn to other means."

The fateful Bloody Sunday in Saint Petersburg in 1905. Hundreds of ordinary people died and thousands were wounded by the soldiers of Czar Nicholas II.

All through the night of this day, which became known in history as Bloody Sunday, processions marched through the streets in the −10°F (−23°C) temperature. This time the purpose of their march was to pick up bodies, load them into coffins, and return them to their families.

Chapter / Three

Exiled "Koba" Becomes "Stalin"

After Bloody Sunday, the Russian people were not the same. They had complained before, they had marched before, and they had kept up some hope for peaceful change. But the news of hundreds of deaths and injuries on that one day destroyed the little hope they had left. Now they fought back with indignation, fear, and horror. Some workers went on strike, some soldiers deserted, some peasants seized land.

The revolution grew. Students, professors, doctors, and lawyers joined in. Railroad workers struck, and public transportation came to a halt. Bakers struck, and there was no bread. Farmers demonstrated, and their animals were left to starve to death. Spies for both sides sneaked in and out of meetings. Terrorists carried out orders to kill, to set fires, to plant bombs.

One story told about Koba says that he climbed a lamppost to shout words of encouragement to the mobs in the street. He then threw homemade bombs into the line of soldiers. When the soldiers started after him, he dashed into a hotel. As they pushed their way into the hotel, he escaped through a cellar passageway.

The revolutionaries needed to work together on plans and goals. Workers, soldiers, and peasants formed councils called soviets.

Worried about the continued unrest, the czar assured the people that they did not need soviets. He promised an election. The subjects could choose representatives to the Duma, a group like a parliament.

Koba scorned the idea. He said the people did not want the Duma. "Comrades, we need only three things," he said. "First, arms! Second, arms! Third, arms!"

Czar Nicholas kept his promise to hold an election for representatives to the Duma. But then he ignored those representatives. Instead he attacked subjects who criticized him. He ordered his soldiers to arrest anyone who spoke out against him or complained about a government regulation. Thousands of workers and peasants were arrested and exiled to Siberia or killed.

Koba became a delegate to the Social Democratic Labour Party Congress. He was rewarded with a visit to his hero, Vladimir Lenin, head of the party.

Lenin believed that a revolution was necessary to break the blind obedience of the people to the priests and the czar. How could untrained, uneducated, unequipped peasants and workers defeat troops of experienced soldiers? First, said Lenin, the people must be convinced that they are fighting for justice. Second, they must always support each other. Third, they must learn how to run, hide, and attack unexpectedly.

Koba soon became an expert revolutionary. He would disappear for a few days and then reappear with a different name. He moved from a house to an apartment and on to another house. He was always just a step ahead of the police. Some historians wonder how he could have escaped so often and how he could have supported Ekaterina and Yakov, his infant son.

Koba was brokenhearted when Ekaterina died

from pneumonia in the spring of 1907. Her death destroys me also, he said to Iremashvili. "This creature softened my stony heart. She is dead, and with her have died my last warm feelings for all human beings." Koba sent Yakov to live with Ekaterina's family. The boy and his father did not see each other for many years.

Koba did not have time to mourn. Carrying on a revolution is something like pushing a heavy truck up a mountain. Many people must push as hard as they can to get it going, and then they have to keep pushing. If they stop to take a rest, the truck will roll back and crush them. If the revolutionaries stopped running and hiding, they could be arrested. If they stopped urging the peasants and workers to demonstrate, the struggle would falter.

The Bolsheviks needed money—and lots of it. They had to buy food and clothing, guns and ammunition, printing presses and paper. They had to pay salaries to full-time workers like Koba.

Lenin had the answer. He called it expropriation. That meant armed holdups. We will be thanked later, he said, when the people realize that their money has bought a society where all people have everything they need.

In 1907, when he was 28, Koba may have been involved in a famous "expropriation" in Tiflis. At 10:30 on the morning of June 26, the chief cashier of the state and two armed policemen signed for two heavy mail sacks at the Tiflis post office. They hauled them to a carriage and, with a guard of 18 mounted police, proceeded to the bank. As they rode along, someone threw a bomb from the roof of a nearby palace. Then six more bombs were thrown. Two guards were killed outright; others were flung from their horses, wheels were blown from the carriage, and horses screamed and reared. More than 50 passersby fell to the ground, wounded or dead.

Then survivors saw a policeman rush away with the bags. Minutes later they discovered that the "policeman" had been a Bolshevik in disguise.

Shortly after, Koba left for Baku, an oil-producing city on the Caspian Sea. There he organized the workers and created a publication for them. He represented them in negotiations with the government, demanding more pay and shorter hours. When he was not successful in these demands, he led the workers in strikes. At one time, 47,000 oil workers were on strike.

Then the police arrested Koba for working against the government. He was put in jail.

The prison at Baku was one of the worst in the country. Some 1,500 prisoners were enclosed in a space designed for 400. In winter it was bitterly cold; in summer people crowded at the barred windows to gasp for air.

Jail discipline was "open." Inmates were locked in only at night. Some escaped, of course. However, those who tried to escape had to sneak by a permanent gallows, which was used freely by the guards.

Koba's arrest was the beginning of a long pattern of arrest, exile, escape, arrest:

1908—arrest and exile to Siberia
1909—escape
1910—arrest and exile to Siberia
1911—end of exile, another arrest and exile
1912—escape from exile, another arrest and exile, another escape from exile
1913—arrest and exile

After one arrest, Koba was taken by train and dogsled across thousands of miles of wilderness to Kureika. This village consisted of just 15 huts, where the prisoners lived. Koba was free to hunt

Siberia in winter—a huge, frozen wasteland

and fish, read and write, and visit with other prisoners. Occasionally he was even allowed to visit at another prison camp. He met many other revolutionaries, and they planned to work together after their release.

Did he try to escape from Kureika? Maybe. But he did not succeed. Perhaps the sub-zero temperatures stopped him, or the stinging winds. Perhaps he thought he could not travel thousands and thousands of miles alone in the wilderness. Perhaps the howls of wolves frightened him.

Koba had lots of time to write while in exile, and he produced many leaflets and articles explaining party decisions. He also began a campaign to elect Bolsheviks to the next Duma, and he planned an underground newspaper.

In one article, he complained that the Bolshevik leaders did not give enough authority to local party leaders. He insisted that local leaders should be free to make mistakes or else they would never learn. He used the persuasive language of his seminary training. In the end, he said, the leaders would walk independently, "as Christ walked on the waters."

He also wrote frequently to local party leaders to offer his services. "If the need is great, then, of course, I'll fly the coop," he wrote, apparently sure that he could escape again.

His letters paid off. In February 1912, Lenin named Koba a member of the Central Committee, the ruling committee of the party, even though he was still in exile.

Five days after he received this news, Koba escaped again.

Once he was back in circulation, his first job

was to send Lenin reports on the state of the Bolshevik movement. Lenin spent most of his time outside of the empire because czarist police had authority to arrest him. Koba also wrote articles and editorials for *Pravda,* the daily newspaper of Saint Petersburg.

In one article he wrote:

> . . . all around we see the smashed workers' organizations, suppressed newspapers, editors arrested, broken-up meetings. . . . The patience of a nation has come to an end.
>
> —Stalin

Stalin! No longer Koba, and no longer Iosif Dzhugashvili. He now took the name—which means "man of steel"—by which the whole world would soon know him.

Stalin was arrested for engaging in revolutionary tactics because of his writing for *Pravda.* His punishment was three years of exile at Narym. The police said he could never escape from this frozen wasteland in northwestern Siberia.

Never? Well, Stalin did not escape in the first two months. But then he made his getaway and headed right back to Saint Petersburg. He disguised himself in a variety of ways, and he kept meeting and hiding, writing and hiding, changing homes and hiding, changing disguises and running. His goal was to get Bolsheviks elected to the Duma.

He was not successful. Only 6 Bolsheviks were elected to the 400-member body. The Bolsheviks were not the only revolutionary party at that time. Socialists, liberals, and anarchists—people who wanted no government at all—competed for power. So did members of various nationalistic groups such as the Armenians and Ukrainians.

The police caught up with Stalin again in March 1913. This time they exiled him to Kostino, Siberia, a village very close to the Arctic Circle. Here the temperature in January may reach −80°F (−62°C), and the light of the winter sun barely makes it to the horizon all day.

The records show that Stalin spent most of the winter on a dogsled, traveling to set traps and to collect the captured animals.

Back in the rest of the empire, factory workers were still overworked, peasants were still starving, and Stalin's friends were still leading demonstrations.

Then came the war.

On July 3, 1914, the message swept through

Saint Petersburg that the czar would speak in the great square that day. Right after mass, Nicholas appeared on his balcony. Hundreds of thousands of citizens below him sank to their knees.

"God save the czar!" they shouted.

The czar announced that Germany had declared war on Russia.

Would the Russians now forget their struggle against the czar? Would they fight on his side as he asked them to?

At first many sided with the czar. Young men joined the army. Older men who had left factory jobs in protest returned to work to help produce supplies for the war. Patriotism spread. The czar changed the German-sounding name Saint Petersburg to one that seemed more Russian—Petrograd. (Ten years later, in 1924, the city was renamed Leningrad. But after the fall of communism in 1991, the city once again became Saint Petersburg.)

But the ill-trained and ill-equipped Russian soldiers were no match for the Germans. Soon deserters were coming back by the hundreds with the news that the Russian soldiers were being slaughtered by the Germans.

The czar needed replacements for the dead and

wounded and for the deserters. But he had already drafted all available citizens. Only political prisoners had escaped the draft. The czar called up the prisoners.

In December 1916, Stalin was ordered to go to Krasnoyarsk to be drafted. He was turned down by the draft. Perhaps it was because of his deformed arm, or perhaps he was considered an undesirable person.

Stalin had only a few months of exile left, and he was allowed to spend them in Achinsk, a village farther south. One of his fellow inmates there described him:

> Thick-set . . . with a swarthy face pitted by smallpox, a drooping mustache. . . . Small eyes, hidden under bushy eyebrows, were dull. . . . His speech was dull.

Stalin was a prisoner, and both the war and the demonstrations continued without him. In Petrograd a fatal cycle began. People would crowd in the street chanting "Bread! Bread!" The czar would order his soldiers to fire. The crowds would scatter. Then they would return, more determined than before. Again, the soldiers would attack.

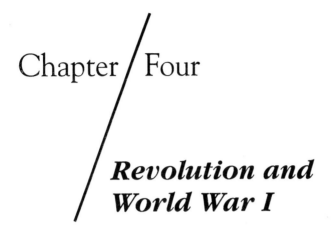

Chapter / Four

Revolution and World War I

When Stalin's exile was over, he left Achinsk with just a small wicker basket holding all his belongings—a few books, some manuscripts, and a few items of clothing. He was invited to live with old friends, the Alliluyevs, in Petrograd.

Nadya, their 15-year-old daughter, was intrigued both by Bolshevik ideas and by Stalin. Some of her schoolmates tried to argue with her that the Bolsheviks were going to destroy Russia, but she refused to listen. Throughout the years, her loyalty won her a special place in Stalin's heart and in his plans.

Petrograd was a run-down city with mud-paved streets, and dozens of closed bakeries, groceries, and other shops. The streets were usually deserted except for small groups of revolutionaries making plans and dreaming dreams, and sometimes staging demonstrations.

Plans and dreams. Plans to overthrow the czar. Dreams of winning over the soldiers. Impossible plans and dreams?

Suddenly the dreams became possible.

On March 11, 1917, the czar's Petrograd troops refused to shoot into lines of demonstrators. Instead they strode along the streets with them, joining in the cries for bread, land, and peace.

At that moment, the city seemed to explode. Demonstrators and soldiers stormed into prisons to release political prisoners. They poured into government buildings, destroying furniture, papers, and records. They raged around the streets, attacking any person who refused to join them. By nightfall there was no order, no law in the city.

News of the riots traveled quickly throughout the empire, and demonstrators in other cities followed the Petrograd example. Czar Nicholas and his family were put under house arrest. Groups of men formed political organizations to bring peace to the country—and to seize control.

Supporters of the Duma in Petrograd quickly set up a temporary government headed by Aleksandr Kerensky, a Socialist lawyer who was well known for his ability to speak forcefully.

Members of the provisional government faced serious problems. They had to create a political climate that would satisfy the people who had risked their lives for the revolution. They also had to continue to fight the war against Germany.

But the new leaders could not work fast enough. Factories closed down from lack of supplies, peasants banded together to steal from landlords, transportation was paralyzed by strikes and lack of equipment, soldiers deserted by the thousands, and the scarcity of food and other necessities created disastrous price increases.

Stalin studied the situation. He decided he had two choices. He could urge Bolsheviks to support the provisional government. Or he could join the Soviet of Workers and Soldiers, a group that had been active in 1905 and now seemed strong again.

He decided to wait and to play the role of peacemaker. He praised the provisional government. He suggested that the Bolsheviks join with the Mensheviks to create one strong party. He praised the Soviet of Workers and Soldiers. And he published his prayer for his country:

Land for the peasants,
Protection for the workers,
And a democratic republic
For all citizens of Russia!

Then came trouble. Lenin had escaped to Finland, accused by the provisional government of
inciting demonstrations. Now he came raging into
Petrograd.

"Why has the party developed no plan to take
command?" he thundered. "Bolsheviks are the only
group tough enough to lead a world revolution."

When Stalin saw that the leading Bolsheviks
were echoing Lenin, he wrote an editorial praising
Lenin's plan:

Under the thunder of the Russian Revolution,
the workers in the west, too, will rise from
their slumber.

The many different groups, parties, and movements that had incited the revolution against the
czar now threatened to overturn the provisional
government.

Lenin announced: "The government is waver-
ing. It must be given the finishing blow at all costs."

On November 17, 1917, at 2:00 in the morning, the Bolshevik Revolutionary Committee ordered their guards to take over Petrograd. At once 20,000 armed Bolsheviks, now called Red guards, or Red soldiers, seized the telegraph agency, state bank, post office, power station, and bridges.

At the czar's Winter Palace, only a few troops, mostly women, were on guard. Few spectators got a glimpse of Kerensky as he escaped in a car flying an American flag.

Twenty-four hours later, most citizens started their day with no knowledge that the Bolsheviks had taken control of their city.

Then the news spread, first through the streets of Petrograd and then throughout the country. Bolsheviks all over the country struck out at the officials of the provisional government.

The Bolsheviks took over office buildings and immediately published laws and regulations:

- Bolshevik leaders had the authority to seize supplies from warehouses, stores, and restaurants.
- All banks and factories belonged to the new government.

- Courts were abolished—revolutionary tribunals would take their place.
- Wage scales would be set by the government.
- Valuable church land would become government property.

The new government was named the Council of People's Commissars. Stalin was made a commissar, a new name for a minister. As commissar of nationalities, Stalin's responsibility was to establish soviets (councils) for minority ethnic groups. This was no small job because minority groups comprised one-half of the population.

Each soviet would elect its own government leaders. Those leaders would be responsible to the national Bolshevik party.

Stalin issued a decree on November 15, 1917, promising equality for all citizens, an end to discrimination against minorities, and the right of provinces to secede, or to break away and become independent.

Still the war with Germany continued—a heavy burden for the people. The villages could not keep up with the demands for food nor the factories with the demands for arms. By the thousands, soldiers were wounded and killed, and by the thousands, they deserted.

Then came a test of the Bolsheviks' popularity. In national elections held to choose representatives to a new parliament, only one-fourth of the votes went to Bolsheviks. They received 9 million votes. A group called the Social Revolutionaries received over 16 million.

Were the Social Revolutionaries going to take control away from the Bolsheviks?

The answer was a big no! In January 1918, as the new parliament prepared to open sessions in a Petrograd palace, Bolshevik troops rushed in. They turned out the lights, declared the assembly dissolved, and sent away everyone except the Bolsheviks. Lenin, Stalin, and a man named Leon Trotsky declared themselves rulers of the country.

They were at the top! But the top of what? The country was still in the midst of civil war. Anti-Bolshevik forces were already organizing to overthrow the new government. The economic system was torn apart by demonstrations, strikes, and lack of transportation. In Petrograd, there were days when bakeries would sell only two slices of bread to a customer. Some days they had no bread at all.

World War I still raged. German soldiers were approaching Petrograd. The new government moved the capital to Moscow, hoping to be safe from the advancing army.

In July 1918, two events hardened Stalin's attitude toward anyone opposed to the Bolsheviks. Lenin was shot and severely wounded by a Social Revolutionary. The chief of the Petrograd secret police was assassinated. Stalin declared, "By instituting open and systematic mass terror, we shall overcome these enemies of the people."

Mass terror! The people could only wonder at the meaning of this phrase. For centuries they had suffered through cruel domination, rebellion, and revolution. To many, Stalin was just one more in the succession of those who promised bread, peace, and land.

Czar Nicholas II, who had offered these same hopes to the people, was shot in July 1918. No one is sure who gave the order to kill the former ruler and his family.

In August, when food supplies ran short in Moscow and Petrograd, Stalin was sent to Tsaritsyn

Commissar Stalin on a mission during the civil war in 1918.

in southern Russia where grain was plentiful. His job was to collect the grain and ship it to the northern cities.

Stalin had to fight for the grain. The Whites, an anti-Bolshevik army, also wanted the grain. The White Army attacked Tsaritsyn just as Stalin arrived.

Stalin did not order an immediate counterattack on the White Army. Instead he ordered a purge—a system of investigations and trials to determine loyalty—of his own soldiers.

The trials did nothing to help move the grain to Moscow. Stalin had two problems. First, most peasants did not want to give up their grain. Second, the Whites had blown up miles of railroad tracks and destroyed many railway cars, leaving no way to ship the grain once it had been seized from the farmers.

Thus Stalin was not able to ship the grain to Moscow. Ten months after Stalin's arrival, Tsaritsyn was taken over by the Whites.

Early in 1919, Stalin was sent to Perm, a city 700 miles (1,120 kilometers) east of Moscow. The Whites there had taken over 300 locomotive engines, 5,000,000 rubles' worth of medical supplies, 150 trainloads of food, and 2,000 rifles. Red Army soldiers were reported to be drunk and disorderly. Stalin's job was to retake the supplies and to discipline the army.

In Perm, Stalin joined the Bolshevik Third Army. From his position there, he became familiar with the work of officers and soldiers. He continued to stress the importance of loyalty to the party above all.

Some months earlier, in November 1918, the First World War had ended with Germany's surrender. But the civil war in Soviet Russia went on.

Chapter / Five

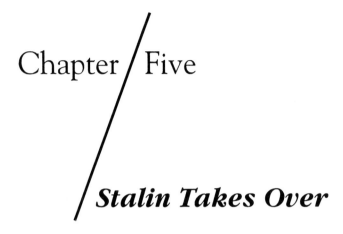

Stalin Takes Over

These were difficult days in Soviet Russia. Bolshevik soldiers, now called Red soldiers, continued to fight against White soldiers and other anti-Bolshevik movements. As in the American Civil War, family members fought on opposing sides. Bloody battles opened new hatreds. The lists of dead and injured grew on both sides.

Many foreign armies had come to Russia to fight against the Germans. But when World War I was over, they did not leave. In fact, after the Armistice, even more French, British, and American soldiers and equipment arrived. These Allies of the capitalistic west were opposed to Bolshevism. They came to support the White Army against the Red Army.

In December 1918, the French landed in Odessa. Stalin was sent there to stop this intervention.

He had heard that some Red Army soldiers had defected, or changed sides, to the Whites. His first action in Odessa was to begin a purge of his own Red Army. He ordered investigations and reports, and he sent hundreds of suspected traitors to firing squads.

He did not attack either the White Army or the French army until he was convinced that his own Red Army was completely loyal to him. When Stalin did attack, he scored a victory. Both the French and the White armies retreated.

On December 31, 1918, more than six weeks after the Armistice, American troops were still stationed in Siberia, suffering the biting winds of the arctic winter. Stalin was enraged by the presence of foreign troops. He never forgave the Allies for staying there.

In March 1919, Stalin married for the second time. Nadya Alliluyev was then 16—less than half Stalin's age—a very pretty girl with dark hair and white skin. Stalin had known her and her family for many years. They moved into a small house in the Kremlin, a group of government buildings in Moscow. A military officer found a few pieces of broken-down furniture for them.

Stalin had no time to settle down. He worked with members to strengthen the party, did routine administrative work to keep offices functioning, continued as commissar of nationalities, and planned battle tactics throughout the country wherever Bolshevik rule was threatened. He built a body of supporters, loyal to him both personally and politically. He continued to gain a reputation for quick judgments and for intolerance toward what he suspected as disloyalty.

Civil war raged in the Soviet Union throughout the spring and summer of 1919. Both the Red and the White armies needed food. Peasants kept watch on the outskirts of their villages. If soldiers approached, they passed on a signal to hide cattle and stored crops.

By the end of 1920, the civil war was over, but the country lay in ruins. Four years of war with the Germans and countless years of revolutionary activity left widespread hunger, unemployment, discouragement, and anger. About 20 million people had been killed as a result of World War I and the civil war. About 1 million had fled the country to escape the Bolsheviks.

In Moscow freezing temperatures caused water mains to burst, leaving holes in the streets. There was no running water or steam heat in the city. People were burning their furniture, doors, and flooring just to keep from freezing to death in the –30°F (–34°C) temperature. There was little to eat but dried fish and moldy bread.

Famine swept across the country as the transportation system failed. In the cities, factories shut down, and a million workers traveled to villages only to find that food was not available there, either. Even those who had been firm supporters of the Bolsheviks the year before were ready to join a new revolt.

When U.S. President Herbert Hoover offered to help Europe with food supplies, Russia asked for a share. The Americans sent food, and 10 million Russians accepted it. Some 100,000 Russians were employed by President Hoover to distribute the food. Afterward, the NKVD, or political police, arrested hundreds of these workers, accusing them of being spies for the United States.

The Tenth Party Congress, in March 1921,

banned all opposition groups within the ruling party.
A Central Control Commission was created to
enforce the ban. Soon the commission was receiving
over 4,000 reports a month of citizens breaking party
rules. Citizens were betraying each other.

The congress ordered the NKVD to keep
secret files on half a million party leaders and
members. The police were to arrest anyone who
appeared to be disrespectful, critical, or uninter-
ested. They were also instructed to identify those
who were strongest in loyalty to Stalin. These men
would be in line for promotion.

Trouble arose in Georgia, Stalin's birthplace.
The Mensheviks had recognized Georgia as a semi-
independent state. Now the Bolsheviks wanted to
unite Georgia, Azerbaijan, and Armenia in
stronger allegiance to the federal government. The
Georgians threatened to secede.

Stalin responded that the Georgians were
being overrun by traitors. He would instruct the
NKVD to conduct a purge of traitors in the Bolshevik party there. He expected the Georgians to
cheer. But most of the people wanted independence, not a Red Army victory.

Then he said that he would arrange for a loan of several million rubles so that Georgians could rebuild their industry. Still they did not cheer. They wanted independence, not loans.

Stalin offered unlimited oil from Baku if the Georgians would merge with the neighboring states of Armenia and Azerbaijan.

Still no cheers. They wanted secession, not union.

Meanwhile, people all over Russia were hungry, cold, unemployed, and fearful for the future. Lenin reasoned that they were not ready for a pure communist economy in which the government owned everything. He instituted a plan, the New Economic Policy. Some businesses were allowed to make a profit. Peasants were allowed to trade some of their produce for manufactured products.

The people reacted with enthusiasm. They pulled their money from hiding places, and they opened shops, bakeries, factories, and restaurants.

On April 3, 1922, Stalin became the general secretary of the Central Committee of the Bolshevik party. Later that month, Lenin was paralyzed by a stroke. Stalin, Grigory Zinovyev, and Lev Kamenev assumed ruling positions in the party—and in the country.

Stalin had often disagreed with Lenin about how much power the individual republics, or states, should hold. Stalin chose this moment, with Lenin ill, to push forward his own idea that the national government should hold power over the states. On October 6, the committee announced that there was "an absolute need for unification" of all states under Moscow.

From his sickbed, Lenin heard the news, and he knew that this was only the beginning of Stalin's takeover.

Lenin had a second stroke on December 16, 1922. Now he knew that he could never return to the Kremlin. He issued a statement: "Comrade Stalin has boundless power in his hands, and I am not certain he can always use this power with sufficient caution."

On January 21, 1924, Lenin died. The Bolsheviks had his body embalmed and placed in a glass-topped coffin. Thousands of mourners followed the funeral procession through the snow-covered streets of Moscow.

Then Lenin's wife announced that her hus-

Lenin (left) and Stalin in 1922

band had not wanted Stalin to take over from him. She had a letter to prove it, she said, and she was going to read the letter to the Central Committee.

When Stalin refused her permission, she threatened to give the letter to the newspapers.

Stalin compromised. The letter would be read at a secret session of the committee.

The secret meeting began. Stalin sat off to one

side, alone, clenching his pipe with jagged yellow teeth. He looked like a typical Russian peasant in his soft-collared tunic with light brown trousers tucked into his boots.

The room was silent as Lenin's criticisms were read. "Stalin is too crude. . . . [We need] someone who differs in all respects from Comrade Stalin . . . who is more tolerant, more loyal, more polite and considerate."

The reader had scarcely finished when Zinovyev, a friend of Stalin's, rose to say that Lenin had been wrong, that Stalin was a magnificently successful and beloved leader.

Immediately others agreed.

Stalin listened as dozens of party members defended him. Then he offered to resign.

The committee refused his offer. They voted 40 to 10 to file and forget the letter.

Later Stalin wrote in his autobiography: "What could I do? Leave my post? . . . I am not a free agent, and when the Party imposes an obligation on me, I must obey."

The party that Lenin had led continued to work to unite the states, the various ethnic groups, and the many political parties of what had once been the empire of the czar. In 1924, the country became the Union of Soviet Socialist Republics (USSR).

At the 14th Party Congress in 1925, Stalin again filled the meeting rooms with his supporters. At one point, a former ally, Lev Kamenev, accused Stalin of holding too much power. Stalin supporters all over the hall shouted him down.

When they had quieted down, Stalin spoke. "It is true, comrades, I am a coarse fellow," he said. They would have to accept that because above all the party needed unity, and he was the person who could bring that unity. They cheered until they were hoarse.

After that meeting, Stalin scheduled regular secret meetings with the Politburo, his advisory group, so that no one could ever again disagree with him in public.

Party purges continued and increased throughout the country. At the 15th Party Congress, 5,000 members were accused of breaking party rules. Three thousand were expelled from the party.

Some of the party faithful were eager to show their loyalty. They changed names of towns and cities, factories, and airports to honor Bolshevik leaders. Stalin's name appeared in several forms: Stalino, Stalinabad, Stalinsk, and Stalingorsk.

Chapter / Six

First Five-Year Plan

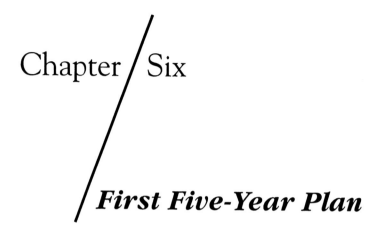

In 1926 Svetlana was born to Nadya and Stalin. She joined a brother, Vasily, who had been born in 1920. Neither parent spent much time with the children. However, they hired nurses and tutors, and thus the children received a lot of attention.

Stalin's nephew, Budu Svanidze, frequently visited in his uncle's home. They enjoyed dinners of borscht (beet soup), Wiener schnitzel (breaded and fried veal cutlet), and sometimes a dessert of baklava (a pastry made with nuts and honey). Often they played dominoes after dinner.

Budu knew that his uncle's father had been a shoemaker, so he was not surprised to discover that his uncle enjoyed working with leather. Vissarion Dzhugashvili had repaired shoes to earn a living;

Iosif Dzhugashvili Stalin, an important political leader, made and repaired shoes as a hobby.

Vissarion had been a strict father, and so was his son. Stalin had adopted the child of an old Bolshevik who was killed in a railway accident. The child, Serge, was afraid of his new father. When Stalin's wife, Nadya, protested that Stalin's punishments were too harsh, Stalin answered that he was going to bring up the boy exactly as he himself had been brought up.

But Stalin was too busy to spend much time at home. The country still had a serious food problem. A plan for collective farms was not working. The plan had seemed simple and sure. Farmers in a village would work together instead of each farmer working for himself. They would share land, labor, and machinery. They would send their crops to a government storehouse, and agents there would distribute the food wherever it was needed.

An unexpected problem was that even the poorest farmers did not want to work on land that belonged to someone else. Most farms had belonged to the same families for generations. Through good times and bad, those plots of land had supplied the farmers' basic needs. When farmers were forced to give up their plots, they lost their enthusiasm for farming.

The kulaks, the wealthier farmers, did not want to share, either. They had made enough money to buy their own machinery and to pay helpers. They had built up productive farms, and they saw no reason to share the wealth they had worked to acquire.

When government agents came to collect grain for the community storehouses, they found very little. The kulaks had dug deep pits and buried it. Then they lied about the success of their harvests.

Stalin worked first on the kulak problem. He had two choices: He could try to persuade the kulaks to cooperate, or he could force them. Persuasion took time. Use of force was a faster way to get food for the hungry citizens. Loyalty to the country was more important than smoothing the feelings of the kulak. He recommended three ways to acquire that loyalty: investigations, threats, punishments.

In December 1927, Stalin issued orders. One: All kulak grain was to be seized immediately. Two: Those who had been hoarding were to be punished. Officials swarmed all over the farms. The

Communist agents dig up bags of grain hidden by kulaks in a cemetery.

kulaks dug deeper pits in which to hide the grain. They made up more complicated stories about their problems with plowing and planting. They lied more about how hard they were working.

The kulaks might be able to hide grain from agents, but surely the peasants who worked on the farms knew where it was hidden. Stalin promised the peasants a share of all the grain they helped the agents to uncover. The hungry peasants accepted the offer. They led agents right to the places where they had helped hide the grain. Once again, Stalin was rewarding citizens for working against each other.

Still the Soviet people were hungry. Threats,

punishments, arrests, and exiles had not created an adequate supply of food.

Stalin next tried a system of rewards. In July 1928, he announced that farmers would receive more money—20 percent more—for their grain.

But the announcement came too late. Planting time had already come and gone. The government could not buy grain that had not been planted! In 1927, farmers had produced over eight billion tons. But in 1928, they produced only six million tons. A bakery that sold nine hundred loaves of bread in one month in 1927 might not have enough flour for even one loaf a month in 1928.

Thousands of agents were sent to the farming areas to find traitors. Their method was to surround a village with police armed with machine guns. Most of the farmers realized immediately that they were beaten, and they agreed to cooperate—to contribute their grain and to report on those who did not.

So, through persuasion and force, skimping and scraping, collecting and delivering, most Soviets survived another difficult winter. Once again, Stalin had led them through a crisis.

Now he looked at his country, and he looked

One of the tragic victims of the Russian famine

at the rest of the world. He thought about the future. He had learned his history well in the village school in Gori and in the seminary at Tiflis. Russian history was punctuated by hundreds of years of foreign invasions, czarism, poverty, oppression, and ignorance.

"We are a hundred years behind the advanced countries. We must make good this lag in ten years. Either we do it, or they crush us," Stalin told his people.

Stalin was not talking about a luxurious life. His own tastes were simple. He usually wore a plain military tunic. In winter, he wore a coat of squirrel and reindeer hide, a garment he had acquired during the revolution. His work habits were rigid. He worked through the night and slept for brief periods during the day.

To move the country forward, in 1928 the Politburo created a five-year plan. Its goal was to replace private ownership with state ownership. The plan included three important goals:

First, the country must industrialize. Workers must concentrate on building factories and machinery. The production of clothing, furniture, and other goods for everyday life was unimportant.

Second, farmers must work together on large collective farms. Private ownership of farms was prohibited.

Third, citizens must forget about profit making. They were to work for the country as a whole, not for themselves. Stalin explained the reasons behind his plan. Now, he said, we have millions of farmers, each plowing a small plot with a wooden plow. What we need are millions of farmers working together on hundreds of large farms with modern equipment.

Now, he continued, we have millions of workers in small, poorly equipped factories, competing to make a profit. What we need are millions of people working together in large modern factories, each person contributing his or her special skill for the good of all.

Stalin promised a golden age where machines would do much of the work, where the standard of living would create comfortable conditions, where jobs in industry would be plentiful, and where a farmer would be almost guaranteed a successful harvest.

But farmers still resisted. Pride in their labor was destroyed when they saw their crops piled into large trucks and shipped off to government store-houses. These farmers secretly brought their crops in from the fields and hid them in deep pits. They planned to dig them up later to feed to their families or perhaps to sell illegally.

When government agents announced that more farms would be collectivized, many farmers said they would rather destroy their property than have it taken away.

Stalin reacted immediately. He declared that all land and crops were government property. Anyone who destroyed government property was guilty of treason. The punishment for treason was death.

Labor camps were set up to imprison farmers who resisted collectivization, workers who seemed less than industrious, and citizens who criticized the government. At the camps, prisoners worked on government projects such as building roads and canals, lumbering, and constructing buildings. Stalin said that these camps taught the inmates the glory of hard work. Those who survived the camp experience said that they were forced into slave labor under the harshest conditions possible—poor food and inadequate housing, improper tools and long hours, backbreaking jobs with little rest.

In all, five million kulaks and peasants refused

to cooperate. In one last burst of rebellion before they were loaded onto trains for Siberia, some kulaks destroyed their property. One estimate is that they killed 20 million horses and thousands of cattle, sheep, and goats.

Historians have wondered what would have happened if Stalin had limited collectivization to farmers who had wanted it. What if groups of farmers had decided on their own to share their land and equipment and labor? What if the government had agreed to lend money to these groups to buy equipment and seed? It might have worked. No one will ever know.

Like the kulaks and peasants, some plant managers and workers objected to the five-year plan. Plant managers were held personally responsible for meeting quotas set by the government. When the quotas were not met, the managers were considered traitors.

There were other reasons why people disliked the plan. For example, the five-year plan goal for production of pig iron was ten million tons a year. Factory workers worked overtime to meet the challenge. In a couple of years, it was clear that they would easily meet the goal. Then Stalin changed the goal. If they can do that well in just two years, he surmised, we can change the five-year goal to seventeen million tons a year.

American Communists visited the Soviet Union in 1929. Stalin scoffed at them for being too timid. He said they should have created a revolution in the United States and taken over just as he and the Bolsheviks had done in the Soviet Union in 1917. He bragged that his communistic country was not suffering from a depression, a difficult economic period, as the United States was at that time. He described the impressive economic growth that resulted from the five-year plan.

The plan did bring considerable growth to Soviet cities. In one generation, the population of Moscow grew from 1.5 million to 5 million. Western Siberia sprouted whole new industrial cities where wastelands once had stood. Some Soviets had a vision of a better country, and they sacrificed for it somewhat as American pioneers had sacrificed for their dreams of a better future.

But not all city dwellers shared these visions. Some could not face the future at all. A Moscow railroad engineer reported as many as a dozen suicides daily as whole families threw themselves in front of his train.

Many sought comfort from the church just as Ekaterina Dzhugashvili and her little son, Soso, had done in their misery years before. For centuries, Russians had found beauty, peace, and security in the great cathedrals, the dramatic chants and prayers, and the awe-inspiring power of the priests.

The priests responded to the suffering of the people by criticizing the government. Stalin well understood the power of the priests. He had to move quickly. Long-robed priests, golden icons, and swinging incense must not distract the people from their work of building a strong Soviet Union.

He issued orders:

- Exile any priest who speaks against Stalin.
- Confiscate and sell the lands, jewels, and other wealth of the churches.
- Turn the church buildings into government offices.
- Do not let the church bells ring, lest the people be reminded of their long-held traditions.

The result of Stalin's attack on the church was anger and increased misery and hunger. Perhaps Stalin thought these were the necessary costs of

Communists make strange use of one of the churches closed for worship—they sort what little grain can be found.

becoming modern and strong.

But was the Soviet Union stronger? In 1930, the answer was no. Everywhere he turned, Stalin faced opposition. To gain support for himself, he published the article "Dizzy with Success." In it, he promised that the terror would stop. He blamed local party officials for the despair, the persecution, and the brutality. Officials who challenged his assertions were exiled or shot.

By the end of 1932, the food situation was desperate. Neither exile nor murder, threats nor punishments had encouraged farmers to plant, plow, or harvest. A farmer who sold a few bales of hay, a cow, or a wagon was accused of trying to make a profit—an illegal act. Branded a traitor, the farmer was punished accordingly.

Starvation threatened the nation. Stalin closed down restaurants and food shops. He started a food-rationing system.

Four years before, in 1928, some energetic and enthusiastic citizens had cheered the introduction of the five-year plan. Now even they were weary and discouraged. They were afraid of hunger, they were afraid of Stalin, and they were afraid of each other.

Chapter / Seven

Second Five-Year Plan

Even party leaders were afraid. Soon unsigned notes were circulating in Kremlin offices. The writers suggested that Stalin be replaced as head of the party. Some spies for Stalin discovered a few of the notes. He ordered that the writers be found and shot. But other leaders refused to allow the shootings.

Even in his own home, Stalin heard the criticism. His widowed mother-in-law lived with Nadya and him. Over and over, she tried to tell Stalin that his plan had caused too much suffering. She had been a peasant herself, she said, and she understood how peasants thought and acted. Stalin finally ordered his mother-in-law to leave their home.

Stalin's wife, Nadya, in a rare photograph

Nadya also spoke against her husband. She openly criticized him in the homes of friends, at family gatherings, and at the university, where she was studying chemical engineering. At a gathering of party workers and leaders in November 1932, Nadya blamed the government for the famine, discontent, and fear in the country.

Stalin listened. Then he shouted at her.

Nadya left the party. She was not seen alive again.

Newspapers reported that she died after a long illness. Many historians believe that she died of a gunshot wound. Some have accused Stalin of killing her. Most believe she committed suicide.

Party leaders who knew both Stalin and Nadya were suspicious, too. There was whispering in the halls and offices of the Kremlin. Boldly, Stalin faced the opposition. "If I become an obstacle to party unity," he said, "I will resign."

Maybe most of the leaders did not believe the rumors. Maybe they were afraid. Whatever the reason, one leader, Vyacheslav Molotov, answered for all of them: "Comrade Stalin, you have our complete confidence."

Meanwhile, living conditions for Soviet citizens became worse. A story was told of a man walking along a village road.

> "Where are you going?" asked a passerby.
> "I'm going to jail," replied the man cheerfully.
> "But you have no guard. Can't you escape?"
> "Yes, I can," answered the man. "But I won't. Because I know that in jail I will be fed."

Stalin rarely left the Kremlin. He carefully

controlled all news about himself. He did not allow photographers near him. Artists drew posters showing him as a handsome young man with a high forehead, bushy mustache, and thick hair. Visitors seeing him for the first time were startled by his coarse, pockmarked skin, low forehead, receding hair, thick lips, and unsightly teeth—some gold, some black.

He would receive visitors in his office, a room with dark green walls and a dark green carpet. On the walls were large portraits of Lenin and Marx. Across one side was a long conference table. On Stalin's desk were a pencil holder and five telephones. Stalin would sit there, silent and heavy lidded, doodling with a pencil while his guests talked.

His private quarters in the Kremlin, where guards lived on the lower floor, were just as plain as his office. The only comfortable furniture in his tiny apartment was one overstuffed chair on which he liked to sit and smoke his pipe. When visitors came, he was eager to talk about Nadya. He showed them her pictures and talked about his grief over her death.

Stalin had no income. He needed none, for he commanded the resources of the country. When he

Stalin at the conference table in his office at the Kremlin

wanted something, he merely asked for it. He always received what he asked for.

Now he realized it was time to make some changes. He announced a whole new series of reforms: Collective farms would receive needed supplies—tractors, seed, tools. Peasants would be allowed to keep half of the profits from the collective farms, and they would be allowed to raise and sell food on small private plots. Every village would have its own theater, sports grounds, library, and cinema. City dwellers were also promised relief. At that time, many families lived in one small room and shared a bath and a kitchen with neighbors. Soon families would have their own quarters.

Factories had been running continuous shifts with no days off. Soon, schedules would include shorter hours and frequent vacation days.

All of the Soviet Union could stand proud now, announced Stalin. In one generation, the people had made enormous progress: Large-scale farms now guaranteed freedom from famine. A new factory system guaranteed both jobs and manufactured goods. The Soviet standard of living was on the rise. And the Soviet Union was strong enough to beat back any attack from the outside. The "outside" was now often referred to as the West. This term included major countries of Europe and North America, most of them strong proponents of capitalism or socialism and opponents of communistic principles.

Now, 1932, was the right time to begin the Second Five-Year Plan. The country had a strong socialist economy. The government owned and operated all essential services. A move toward a communist government now would assure that each citizen earned a fair share of the rewards of a stable economy. Soon, each person could help himself to whatever he needed. The new slogan was: Life is better, comrades, life is happier.

Targets for the Second Five-Year Plan were more realistic. There was a continued emphasis on heavy industry and also an effort to produce consumer goods.

Stalin had industrialized the nation in five years. Now he wanted to make it cosmopolitan in the next five. He began a campaign for a cultural revolution.

His campaign encouraged people to learn to read and write, to pay attention to personal cleanliness, and to act politely toward each other. Women were encouraged to use lipstick and to carry handkerchiefs. Men were advised to dress neatly, behave politely, and speak courteously.

Workers were given every sixth day off, restaurants were reopened, and factories held (compulsory) classes in modern dance.

As a symbol of the new Soviet Union, the most beautiful subway in the world was built in Moscow. Thousands traveled to Moscow to admire the subway's wide corridors, gleaming marble columns, mosaic floors, and beautiful pieces of sculpture.

Church buildings that had been taken over by the government just a few years before now became museums of religious history.

But a group of armed Leningrad youths declared that Stalin had been responsible for the worst terror of the years past and that any new plan would be just as unsympathetic to the people.

Stalin heard the criticism and immediately ordered that the 117 suspects be shot without a trial. He then exiled thousands of party workers in Leningrad, accusing them of allowing the young people to demonstrate.

Soon the Second Five-Year Plan looked like a carbon copy of the first one.

Workers and farmers were pushed to break production records. Reports of seemingly impossible feats were announced by the government. In an average shift, a worker might cut 7 tons of coal; one worker reported that he had cut 102 tons. In an average harvest, an area of land might yield 103 units of sugar beets; one farmer reported a harvest of 300 units.

More! Better! Faster! The orders shot out from Moscow. Criticizing and complaining, the government said, were diseases that spread from worker to worker, attacking the well-being of the factories. The only cure was to get rid of the infected worker—by exile, arrest, or shooting.

Still the infection grew. Factory managers, party leaders, investigators, and other government officials questioned: Should a worker be shot for complaining about factory conditions? Should a man be sent to a labor camp for a record of being tardy? Should a peasant be arrested for refusing to work more than ten hours a day? Some of the questioners were jailed, some were put on trial, and some simply disappeared.

The lives of the people were regulated by the police, not by government officials and party leaders. At the factories, no longer were the police merely investigating the workers and managers; the police were now actually running the industries themselves. In secret trials, thousands of old Bolsheviks were accused of being traitors. They were condemned without proof, and then they were shot. Then the clerks and other staff members who had worked under them were accused of the same crimes, and they were also shot.

Stalin replaced an NKVD chief whom he declared was an enemy of the people. The replacement, Nicolay Yezhov, was especially brutal. One of his first acts was to accuse the former chief of conspiring to poison Stalin.

Then Yezhov ordered more mass arrests, secret trials, and instant executions. He gave orders to NKVD agents throughout the country, demanding the execution of thousands of people. His orders stated the number of people to be killed. He did not include names of suspects or the crimes with which they were charged. His telegram to Frunze, the capital of Kirghizia, read:

> To NKVD Frunze. You are charged with exterminating 10,000 enemies of the people.
>
> —Yezhov

Such telegrams were dispatched at intervals

throughout the Soviet Union. Some historians believe that seven million to eight million people were purged in this way. A few set the figure at more than twenty million.

Stalin was on continual guard against conspiracy and possible assassination. He surrounded the Kremlin with NKVD officers and gave every Politburo member, including himself, a bodyguard. Anyone who lingered in Red Square was swept into an NKVD office, searched, and questioned. Troops were not allowed to carry ammunition when they paraded in Red Square. All visitors to the Kremlin needed special passes, which were inspected at a number of check sites. Stalin told no one, not even his closest associates, of his schedule.

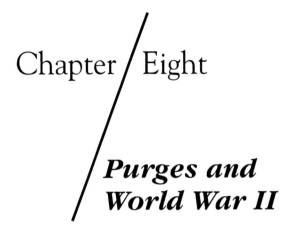

Chapter / Eight

Purges and World War II

No more unemployment. No more discrimination. No more poverty. Stalin's 1936 constitution promised all this and more. The right to vote for all citizens over age 23. New cooperation among all people. Freedom of speech, personal property, and religion. "It is not property status, nor national origin, nor sex, nor office, but personal ability and personal labor that determine the position of every citizen in society," Stalin declared.

But many history books do not even mention this constitution. The years 1936 to 1939 are better known for the Show Trials and the Great Purge.

The Show Trials were hearings of Soviet leaders accused of treason. They are called the Show Trials because the foreign and local press were invited to observe and to report.

Reporters watched as prisoners entered the high-ceilinged, white-walled room in the former Hall of Nobles and faced three judges. Each prisoner told a story of his own disloyalty—some said they had plotted to assassinate Stalin, some said they had worked with foreign governments to overthrow the Soviet Union, some reported having blown up factories and destroyed railroad cars and tracks.

After confessing, each prisoner praised Stalin and asked to be punished:

> Here I stand before you in filth, crushed by my own crime. . . . No matter what my sentence will be, I consider it will be just. . . .

Then the prisoner was declared guilty and sentenced to exile or to death by firing squad.

The same routine occurred, over and over again, as though it were a script for a play. Historians say it was just that. They say that Stalin was insecure around any government leader who might disagree with him. They say that he had confessions written, which he forced the prisoners to sign, memorize, and repeat at the trials.

Why would a man confess to something he had not done? Perhaps some confessed because they were so dedicated to communism that they believed they must have done something wrong simply because they were accused. Perhaps some were confused, uncertain, easily led to make some sort of confession. And perhaps some thought that if they told the astounding stories written for them, the judges would be suspicious and would search for the truth.

One thing is certain. Many people were tortured into making false confessions. Researchers report that prisoners were interrogated for as long as 48 hours without food or sleep. They were burned with cigarettes, kicked, punched, slapped, and beaten with heavy instruments until they fell onto the floor, bloody and unconscious.

One method of torture did not involved physical pain at all. The prisoner was told that members of his family would be tortured if he did not confess.

Many foreign reporters were suspicious because all the prisoners confessed and all asked for punishment. These reporters took careful notes and then did some investigating. They found that some of the prisoners had told stories that could not have been true.

Defendants at a Show Trial listen to the accusations against them.

For example, one prisoner admitted to a meeting with another suspect at a certain hotel in Copenhagen. A reporter said that he found no record of that hotel. Another prisoner said that he had flown from Berlin to Oslo in 1935. The reporter said that he checked the Oslo records and found that no plane had landed there during the month the prisoner said he had flown there.

Stalin also ordered trials that were not open to the public. These secret trials, part of the Great

Purge, were necessary, he said, because certain people were threatening the progress of the country.

Enemies and *wreckers* became key words in the 1930s. Stalin again requested that every citizen watch every other citizen for evidence of disloyalty to the government. *Pravda* warned against enemies:

> We know that assembly lines do not stop by themselves, machines do not break by themselves, boilers do not burst by themselves. Someone's hand is behind every such act.

Historians estimate that four million to five million people were arrested between 1936 and 1939 in the Great Purge. In Moscow alone, a thousand people were shot on some days.

A Soviet historian, Roy Medvedev, later studied records, pamphlets, periodicals, and other printed materials of that period. He interviewed hundreds of people to learn about the Show Trials and the Great Purge. He reported that people from all walks of life were arrested, exiled, and shot. His list included members of the Central Committee, government officials, army commanders, teachers, farmers, police, musicians, and actors.

Musicians! Actors! How could their work be

suspicious? One story says that Stalin saw a ballet in which the dancers portrayed drunken Russians and foolish Georgians. Immediately, he issued a decree that plays, dances, and operas should show Soviets only at their best. After that decree, the story goes, half the musical artists stopped producing. The other half changed their presentations to depict all Soviets as hardworking and serious characters.

Nikita Khrushchev, who was the leader of the Soviet Union after Stalin's death, reported seeing Stalin with more than 350 "death lists" between 1937 and 1938. These lists contained names of people arrested for disloyalty. Khrushchev said that Stalin glanced through them, initialed them, and sent them back. Those initials spelled imprisonment or death for the people whose names were listed. Records indicate that over 44,000 people may have been sentenced in this way.

Not all who confessed were killed. Some were sent to labor camps in Siberia. Some lived long enough to write about their lives there. One wrote:

. . . it took twenty to thirty days to turn a healthy man into a wreck. Working in the camp mine sixteen hours a day . . . sleeping in a torn tent at sixty below zero . . .

Another wrote:

. . . in the morning they brought a piece of black bread, a spoon of sugar, and boiling water . . . supper was a few spoonfuls of groats [wheat kernels] and boiling water . . .

How could any man order such suffering and so many deaths? Some say that Stalin was bored by human existence. Some say that murder was his only justification for living. Others say that he believed that purges were necessary to allow him to lead the country to a communistic society. Still others say that he believed that his crimes were insignificant because he had accomplished so much good for the country.

Joseph Davies, United States ambassador to the Soviet Union at that time, was confused. "A child would like to sit on his [Stalin's] lap and a dog sidle up to him. It is difficult to associate his personality with these purges."

No one knows why the Soviet citizens were not able to stop the trials and the executions. One possible answer is that those who questioned Stalin's authority soon found themselves on the stand, accused of treason. Another possibility is that many people simply did not realize the extent of the purges. Others say that citizens believed in Stalin because they had been taught to follow him blindly. Perhaps some people had higher living standards than their parents did under the czar and during the revolutionary upheavals. Thus, they were content to leave controversy alone. Also, many were uneducated, and they did not have any idea that they might be able to participate in government. It appears that many believed Stalin when he announced that his strict measures were necessary to fight Fascists and foreign spies.

Stalin announced the end of the purges at the 18th Party Congress in March 1939. He stated then that the country was free of spies and traitors.

He cited statistics that he said proved that the purges had increased loyalty to the government. In 1937, some Soviet traitors were shot, he said. In the elections after those shootings, 98.6 percent of the votes went to the Communists. In 1938, more traitors were shot. After that, 99.4 percent went to Communist officials. He neglected to say that there was only one candidate—a Communist party one—for each position on the ballot in those elections.

Enjoy! Enjoy! Stalin encouraged the people to enjoy the prosperity that his two five-year plans had brought. Enjoy the abundant food, the opportunity to travel, the material goods, the luxurious homes. Enjoy the riches of communism.

He said the people had produced more grain, laid more railroad track, and built more machinery than ever before. He claimed the Soviet Union's industrial output was ahead of that of capitalistic countries such as the United States, Great Britain, France, and Germany.

As Stalin made plans to continue building up the Soviet Union, he discovered a serious problem. Because of the purges, most of the experienced government leaders were gone. So were many business and agricultural leaders. So were teachers and scientists and thousands of workers and farmers.

Meanwhile, in Europe, World War II was beginning. In March 1938, the Germans invaded Czechoslovakia, a small country on Russia's border.

In August 1939, Stalin met with Adolf Hitler's foreign minister in Moscow. The Soviet Union and

Germany signed agreements promising not to attack each other. Stalin saw both economic and military advantages to these agreements. The Stalin/Hitler pact shocked the world. Stalin's supporters felt betrayed. The two political systems—communism and fascism—had always been completely opposed to each other.

After the signing, Stalin was host to the Germans at a dinner in the Kremlin Grand Palace, a former home of the czars. Flowers, electric candles, gilded silverware, waiters dressed in white—the dinner was magnificent. Stalin stood at the chair of each guest as that guest was given a special toast by Soviet foreign minister Vyacheslav Molotov. Both Soviets and Germans declared the meeting a success.

A few days later, the Germans invaded Poland from the west, and the Soviet army invaded Poland from the east. World War II had begun. Britain and France declared war on Germany.

Stalin sent Red Army troops into Latvia, Estonia, and Lithuania, three small countries on the Russian northwestern border. The troops were a buffer between the Soviet Union and possible invaders from the west.

He asked Finnish leaders to allow the Soviet

Officials smile for the camera at the signing of the infamous Stalin/Hitler pact in August 1939.

Union to build a naval base on Finnish territory. The Finns refused. On November 30, 1939, the Soviets invaded Finland by land, sea, and air. In March 1940, Finland surrendered to Russia after a brave resistance.

Then rumors began to fly that Germany would attack the Soviet Union. Still, the Soviet Union did not prepare for an invasion. But on June 22, 1941, 3,500 German tanks, 4,000 German airplanes, and 190 divisions of German soldiers attacked the Soviet Union. They invaded towns and villages, bombed cities, and captured vast

quantities of arms, ammunition, and fuel. Totally
unprepared for the attack, hundreds of Soviet soldiers and civilians were killed or taken prisoner.

On July 3, Stalin spoke to his people. Loud-
speakers in city streets blared his message. Our
country has been attacked by fiends and cannibals,
he said, but we will overcome by working together.
He announced that he was now supreme comman-
der of the Soviet military establishment. He
warned that Soviet traitors would be dealt with
severely. Citizens in the western part of the country, who were forced to retreat from the Germans,
had orders. They were told to burn their fields so
that no food would be available to invaders. They
were told to leave nothing for the enemy, not a sin-
gle engine or railway car, not a pound of grain or
gallon of fuel. They were ordered to blow up
bridges, destroy roads, damage telephone and telegraph lines, and set fire to forests and stores.

Stalin traveled from his suburban dacha, or
vacation home, to Moscow on July 4, and after that
was seen only two or three times a year during the
course of the war. It is believed that he spent most
of his time in a bomb shelter in the Kremlin. The
shelter was 115 feet (45 meters) below ground and

protected by a maze of automatic steel doors and secret tunnels, plus a number of warning systems. Military officers worked in adjoining rooms.

In that same year, Svetlana planned to study literature at a university. Her father objected. "No, you'd better get a decent education. Study history," he advised. She took his advice. Vasily, although an alcoholic, was a major in the air force.

Many Soviet citizens welcomed the Nazis when Hitler invaded the Ukraine. Some 400,000 peasants who had been members of the Red Army deserted to the German side. The Ukrainians sought freedom from the government that had murdered their kulaks and peasants and had forced collectivization. They asked for Hitler's protection.

Hitler answered with imprisonment and death. Nazis shipped millions of prisoners to the west. Some were sent to concentration camps; others, to forced labor camps.

Stalin named himself premier, head of the government. He needed supplies desperately, and he asked the United States and Britain for help, He asked for tanks, planes, destroyers, army boots, shellac, and medical supplies. He was angry that he did not receive all that he asked for.

Yakov, Stalin's son, after his capture by the Germans

Then Stalin learned that the Germans had captured Yakov, his and Ekaterina's son. The Germans were willing to trade the soldier for some German prisoners. Stalin did not reply. Some historians believe that Yakov died in a prison camp. Others say that he lived in the Soviet Union after the war and never again saw his father.

On October 16, 1941, Stalin ordered a mass evacuation of Moscow. Posters were displayed everywhere: "All citizens whose presence is not needed are hereby ordered to leave. The enemy is at the gates."

By November, the German army had reached Moscow. To be safe from Nazi bombing, the Kremlin leaders held their scheduled meeting in the Moscow subway station. After that meeting, citizens gathered in the station to listen to Stalin. German guns rumbled in the distance as he spoke.

Stalin ordered party leaders to stop antireligious activities. He called on the Orthodox church to join him in the struggle against the Nazis. He called on Soviet factory workers to produce military supplies.

In December 1941, Japan attacked the United States at Pearl Harbor. The United States and Britain declared war against Japan. Soon after that, the United States declared war on Germany.

In May 1942, Stalin asked the United States and Britain to help force Hitler to withdraw some of his troops from the Soviet Union. Stalin's plan was to establish a second front. He wanted United States and British forces to attack the Germans in northern France. Then Hitler would be compelled to move some of his troops from the Soviet Union to meet that attack in Europe. President Roosevelt and Prime Minister Churchill answered that they needed their military strength in other places at that time. They said they would honor Stalin's request as soon as they were able. Stalin was angry.

A few months later, Stalin again asked for help. He wanted aircraft guns, aluminum sheeting for airplane construction, and rifles. Churchill responded that Britain did not have enough supplies to share. Stalin replied that he thought that Britain was stalling. He accused the British of expecting the Soviet Union to fight the most difficult battles alone.

Stalin reminded the Allies that they had promised to open a second front in France. Again, they said they would, but they did not say when. Stalin asked how he could be expected to believe them this time. There was no answer.

In August 1942, the Germans attacked Stalingrad. On the second day of the battle, 40,000 Soviet soldiers were killed in a night air raid. German tanks and troops then moved through the city, demolishing block after block of buildings. But the people did not surrender.

Military leaders in Stalingrad cabled Moscow for reserves of men and equipment. Stalin answered that they did not need more supplies;

they only needed more courage. "Don't move one step back," he told them.

By November, Hitler probably believed that Stalingrad would fall to the Nazis at any moment. He was in for a big surprise.

Suddenly Stalin ordered a massive assault on Stalingrad. The Red Army fought with ferocious bravery. The Stalingrad workers armed themselves and joined the soldiers.

The Germans were neither dressed nor equipped for the Stalingrad winter. They were frostbitten, without supplies, half-starved, wounded. Two out of every three German soldiers died in the –23°F (–31°C) temperature, in the storms of ice and snow. They suffered three long months before they retreated. They left behind 300,000 dead or captured. And they left thousands of Red soldiers, encouraged by the victory and brimming over with praises of Stalin.

The battle of Stalingrad was a turning point. Now the Germans began to retreat from other fronts, too. In cities and towns all over the Soviet Union, German soldiers began a westward move-ment with the Red Army right behind them. One by one, Soviets recaptured their cities. As each city was retaken, Stalin sent NKVD agents there to execute anyone who was suspected of having collaborated with, or helped, the Germans.

In 1944, Stalin ordered a powerful new offensive. He retook the Crimean Peninsula. One of his first acts after this victory was to punish 500,000 civilians who had worked for the Germans. He exiled them to Siberia.

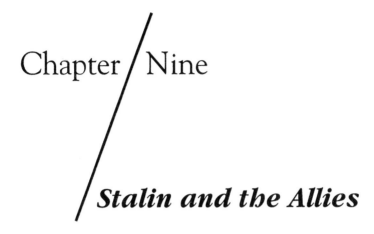

Chapter / Nine

Stalin and the Allies

Prior to World War II, Stalin had had little to do with leaders of other countries. Suddenly, he was forced to discuss, plan, and negotiate with a number of different leaders. The stories of these meetings reflect Stalin's feelings of distrust, suspicion, and hostility.

One of his first important conferences with President Roosevelt and Prime Minister Churchill was held in Tehran, the capital of Iran, in November 1943.

For the Soviet people, Stalin had dressed like a peasant or worker. For the rest of the world, he wanted to dress more formally, so he had new clothes made for the conference. No more drab gray-brown. He wore dark blue. No more soft tunic buttoned to the neck. He wore a stiff military jacket with white stars on the shoulders. No more baggy trousers tucked into soft felt knee boots. He wore tailored navy blue trousers with red stripes down the sides and shiny leather shoes. His hat was covered with gold braiding.

He was now Generalissimo Stalin, a symbol of military strength. However, he retained some simple rural attitudes. At a banquet in Tehran, he asked a dinner partner for help. "This is a fine collection of cutlery. It is a problem which to use. You will have to tell me."

At the conference, Roosevelt, Churchill, and Stalin discussed ways to work together to end the war. They also decided to establish the United Nations.

The war continued. The Red Army fought the Germans in the Soviet Union and in Poland. The Allies fought in Italy, the Pacific Islands, France, and Japan.

In October 1944, the Allies defeated Germany in Hungary, Yugoslavia, Bulgaria, Czechoslovakia, and Poland. Stalin sent in Red Army troops. He also sent in Communist leaders to set up new governments that would be loyal to the Soviet Union.

The Red Army came prepared to stay in these countries. They brought everything from secretaries to military police, from food and clothing to tanks and guns. The Allies called these countries Soviet satellites, unquestioning followers of the Soviet Union.

The war was almost over when Stalin, Churchill, and Roosevelt met at Yalta, a Crimean port, in February 1945. What a glorious conference that might have been! A conference to plan peace, not war! But even at the opening session, Stalin spoke of suspicion and distrust: "The danger in the future is the possibility of conflicts among ourselves."

The overriding conflict concerned the fate of a defeated Germany. The other leaders wanted to divide Germany into four occupied zones, with the Soviet Union, the United States, Great Britain, and France each responsible for one zone. When Stalin refused to admit France into this plan, the other leaders agreed to make a zone for France out of their zones.

Another conflict was over Poland. Against the arguments of the others, Stalin insisted that the Red Army stay in Poland. Another conflict concerned Japan. Stalin agreed to enter the war against Japan only after the other leaders agreed to give Russia some Japanese islands after the war.

Stalin was confident about himself. However, he admitted that he was less than confident about his people in comparison to Westerners. He said, "Ours [generals] still lack breeding and their manners are bad. Our people have a long way to go."

On April 12, President Roosevelt died. His vice president, Harry Truman, took over.

The Germans were going to lose the war. There was no question about that. Two questions remained: When will the surrender take place? Which army will be the first to enter Berlin?

Both the Soviets and the Americans were close to Berlin. But they knew the people in the German capital would put up a strong resistance. President Truman estimated that 100,000 soldiers might be killed in the final rush. He decided to wait for reinforcements. Generalissimo Stalin did not wait. One million Soviet soldiers were killed in that Soviet push to Berlin. The Soviet army entered the city on April 21, 1945.

Germany surrendered on May 7, and the lead-

Churchill, Roosevelt, and Stalin at the famous Yalta conference in 1945—another missed opportunity for world peace.

ers of the Soviet Union, the United States, and Britain made plans to meet again to discuss peace.

At the Potsdam Conference in July 1945, Stalin was strong in his opinions and mentally alert. However, he was beginning to show the effects of hard work and age. His skin had an unhealthy sallow look. His hair was turning gray. But he alone was head of the country. He trusted no one but himself in matters of importance.

Stalin announced to Truman and Churchill

that Germany owed the Soviet Union $10 billion for war damages. This money would pay for homes, schools, machinery, railroads, power plants, factories, and hospitals destroyed by the war.

Truman and Churchill objected. How could Germany rebuild its own badly damaged country if it paid all this to the Soviet Union? Stalin replied that the rebuilding was Germany's problem, not the Soviet Union's.

Stalin had ordered his soldiers to dismantle some of the industrial plants in Germany, and he had the machinery shipped to the Soviet Union. Truman and Churchill objected, saying that in the interests of peace, Germany should not be punished so harshly. Stalin continued to expropriate the machinery.

The big news at the Potsdam Conference was that the United States had an atomic bomb.

The United States dropped an atomic bomb on Hiroshima, Japan, on August 6, 1945. On August 8, the Soviet Union declared war on Japan. Stalin sent 1.5 million soldiers to the Far East. On August 9, the United States dropped an atomic bomb on the Japanese city of Nagasaki. On August 14, Japan surrendered.

Now Stalin could concentrate on his own country again. But the situation was a disaster. About 27 million soldiers and civilians had died. About 25 million citizens were homeless. The Soviets were weary and discouraged. Their farms were wastelands, their factories little more than rubble, and their homes and other buildings had been destroyed.

The government needed money. Stalin again asked that the Allies force Germany to pay war damages to the Soviet Union. The Allies again rejected his request.

As he had in the 1920s, Stalin told his people that a weak Soviet Union might tempt stronger countries to invade. He turned to the satellite countries. He would use their resources of industry, agriculture, and workers to rebuild the Soviet Union.

He turned to them for protection, too. The satellites would serve as a buffer against any attacks from Western Europeans.

Churchill was concerned about the pressure that Stalin was putting on the satellite countries. He heard about a Soviet push to develop an atomic bomb. He made his famous Iron Curtain speech. We do not have a world working together for peace, he said. Stalin has placed an iron curtain between his lands and ours. This iron curtain prevents us from working together. It creates suspicion and distrust.

In January 1947, President Truman echoed these thoughts. He declared that there was a "cold war," a war of words and ideas, being waged by the Soviet Union against its former allies.

Stalin ordered a propaganda offensive against the United States, calling upon workers in all countries to protest American imperialism in Latin America and China. In September 1947, Soviet minister Andrey Vyshinsky attacked United States policy. He said it was leading to war.

In March 1948, the United States, Britain, and France united their separate German sections into one zone called the Federal German Republic, which became known as West Germany. Stalin named the Soviet-occupied zone the German Democratic Republic, or East Germany.

The city of Berlin, which lay deep within East Germany, had also been divided by the Allies. East Berlin fell under the control of the Soviet Union, while the Americans, British, and French held the western part of the city.

Stalin's philosophy toward Germany differed

considerably from that of the Americans and their allies. Stalin wanted to punish the Germans for the devastation they had caused during the war. The Western democracies, however, believed that the German economy should be built up, and that the German people should be taught democratic principles. A prosperous and democratic new Germany would be the best safeguard for world peace, they believed.

Residents of West Berlin, living under a capitalistic system, were more prosperous than those of East Berlin. Stalin wanted to stop this competition and to control the entire city. On June 24, 1948, he closed all the highways, railroads, and waterways that led to Berlin. Transportation into the city was impossible except for a narrow air lane unintentionally left free.

Stalin must have been surprised when the Allies began to fly in materials on the one airstrip that was not controlled by the Soviet Union. Within a few days, the Allies were flying up to 4,500 tons of supplies to West Berlin.

Stalin continued his blockade. The Allies continued their airlift. Finally, after almost a year, Stalin revoked the blockade.

Stalin's leadership dominated the satellite

countries, now often called the Iron Curtain countries. Only one country, Yugoslavia, refused to follow his commands.

In March 1948, Stalin wrote to Marshal Joseph Tito, leader of Yugoslavia, demanding that he follow Stalin's orders. Tito refused again. In June, the Soviet Union broke diplomatic relations with Yugoslavia.

To ensure that other satellites would not follow Tito's lead, Stalin ordered a purge of dissidents, those who disagreed with him, in these states. At their trials, many of the accused confessed to being spies for the United States. The United States denied knowing anything about them.

Throughout this period, Stalin seemed to feel most at home in one of his vacation retreats, where he wandered alone for hours in the dark pine forests. He did entertain a little in his Kremlin apartment. His guests were mostly old friends who ate and drank with him. When Svetlana married, Stalin invited the couple to live in the apartment above his. When Svetlana declined, Stalin was angry.

He was too busy to be angry for long. He turned his attention to countries that lay to the east. Korea had been split into two zones at the end of the war. In 1950, the Red Army sent advisers, tanks, and weapons to North Korea. Soon, banners appeared on the streets: LONG LIVE STALIN! and THE SOVIET GOVERNMENT IS THE HIGHEST FORM OF DEMOCRACY.

In June 1950, the North Korean army, aided by the Soviet Union, invaded South Korea. The American army went to the support of South Korea.

After two years of fighting, with thousands killed on both sides, Korea remained divided. The Soviet Union and the United States were greater enemies than ever.

In Germany, the bitterness continued. Stalin insisted that reunification could not take place until the Germans promised not to join with the West against the Soviet Union. President Truman refused to accept this condition.

Stalin built up an East German police force of 50,000 men, the size of a small army.

President Truman then rearmed West Germany. West Germany joined the North Atlantic Treaty Organization (NATO), guaranteeing to help the West in the event of attack by the Soviet Union.

Once again, the United States and the Soviet Union had opposed each other in another country. Once again, neither had won.

The cold war spread to nearly every corner of the world. Whatever side the United States took in a nation's affairs, the Soviets almost always took the opposing position—and vice versa. For the next 40 years, the two military superpowers played out their conflicts on a world chessboard, and the smaller nations were their pawns.

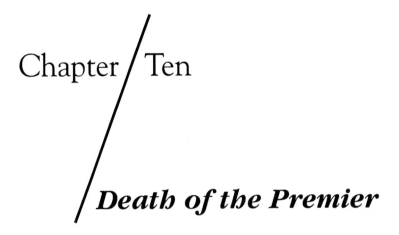

Chapter / Ten

Death of the Premier

On December 21, 1949, all of Red Square was a birthday party for 70-year-old Stalin. Huge balloons bearing his picture floated over buildings draped in red. Guns blared in salute. Presents poured in from all over the country: embroidered cloth, swords, tankards, carpets—so many presents that a museum was later built to house them all.

Poets wrote that Stalin was the sun, the lord of creation.

A novelist predicted that new calendars would begin with Stalin's birth, not with the birth of Christ.

Communist leaders shouted their praises:

Glory to Stalin!

East Berlin glorifies the dictator on his 70th birthday.

Without Stalin, we would not have world
peace!
Without Stalin, we would not have food or
industry!
Stalin has brought us into the atomic era!

Hundreds gathered in Red Square. They
looked up at white-headed Generalissimo Stalin,
waving and smiling from his balcony. They waved
back, and they cheered and applauded.

Then many went home to another Moscow

winter of long working hours and low wages, chilly rooms, and cabbage soup and potatoes three times a day.

A typical factory worker might have wondered: Where was hope? He might have been inspired 20 years earlier by the first Five-Year Plan. Perhaps he had given up a comfortable Moscow life to pioneer in the wastelands of Siberia in 1928. Perhaps he had believed Stalin, that "the individual will be freed from concern about his daily bread." But maybe he had returned from cold, hunger, and overwork in Siberia to cold, hunger, and unemployment in Moscow.

Then, in 1938, he and his wife might have worked 12-hour shifts, six days a week to build up the Soviet economy. They might have accepted Stalin's words: "A man will not be haunted by fear of being deprived of work, home, and bread." But perhaps they had watched in horror as many of their friends and neighbors were arrested and sent to labor camps.

Ten years later, in 1948, he and his wife, their two married daughters and their husbands, and their four grandchildren might have been living in a six-room apartment in Moscow with twenty-five other people. They might have been sharing one kitchen and one bathroom. Could they still believe Stalin's words, that "our party intends a new upsurge of the economy"?

Each morning, this worker would read the banners at the entrance to the factory: GLORY TO WORK! CARRY OUT THE PLAN AHEAD OF SCHEDULE!

Inside the plant, he might have tried to block out the deafening noises, to ignore the stifling heat from the inefficient furnaces, to coax worn-out tools into working order. Each evening, he would return to his crowded apartment. Could he believe in the glory of work?

Many researchers have tried to learn more about Stalin's personal life. Some writers have said that Stalin was silly at parties. They say that a favorite game of his was to have guests guess how many degrees it was below zero. Losers had to drink as many glasses of vodka as the number of degrees they had guessed wrong. Another game was to estimate the size of a room. The forfeit was the same as that of the temperature game.

Some biographers say that Stalin often went on and on, telling stories about his life while his guests struggled to keep their eyes open.

Biographers have also wondered what Stalin thought about himself as a leader. It might be said that he thought he was worth at least 33 tons of pure copper. That is what he ordered to be sent to the Volga-Don Canal to be made into a 100-foot-high (39 meters) statue of himself.

Soviet families made thousands of smaller statues for their own use. Any material that could be molded or carved was used—plaster, hammered iron, bronze, wood. They were painted, sprayed, gilded, decorated in many different ways. Millions of tinier statues of the Soviet leader were stamped out by machines.

On October 5, 1952, the 19th Party Congress opened with an eight-hour-long speech by party leader Georgi Malenkov. The entire speech was in praise of Stalin. Every time Malenkov spoke Stalin's name, the audience shouted and applauded. Stalin sat on the stage, looking like a kindly grandfather, smiling slightly. He answered the applause in Soviet style, by applauding gently himself.

On the last day of the congress, Stalin warned against the dangers of capitalism. As long as there were capitalist countries, he warned, there would

be conflicts and war because the capitalist governments are based on greed. Once again, the audience rocked with applause.

After the congress, Stalin planned the most
massive purge of his career. He planned investigations of the entire government, starting with the
highest levels and working down through the
ranks.

He limited the number of Jews who could
attend each college. Jewish military officers began
to realize that they would not be promoted. Jews
were not allowed to become party members. Jewish
doctors found that their patients would not accept
prescriptions from them. The patients had been
encouraged to suspect poison from Jewish physi-
cians.

Stalin ran a police state. Not only did the
police run the factories, but they also had charge of
railroads, dams, waterways, harbor facilities,
nuclear energy programs, and all the work on the
atomic and hydrogen bombs. The police grew in
numbers and power. Soon they had their own tank
corps, artillery units, and air force.

In January 1953, an announcement was made
that several Kremlin doctors had tried to murder

three marshals, an admiral, a general, and two government leaders.

One doctor, Vladimir Vinogradov, Stalin's personal physician, was charged with plotting against the government. He confessed to this crime. Later, historians found evidence that he had been innocent, but that he was chained and beaten until he wrote the confession.

One historian writes that the other doctors were beaten into unconsciousness as well. When they revived, they were told to sign confessions already written for them. Then they were beaten again. Then more confessions were demanded. It is reported that Stalin said to one of the torturers, "If you do not obtain confessions, we shall see that you are shortened by a head."

Suspicion and terror spread. If the doctors had been in a conspiracy, what about lawyers, officials, teachers? More and more accusations were made, and more and more confessions were signed.

In offices, one method of terror was common. A worker would be told that he was assigned to a special secret mission. "I can't tell you where I'll be," he would tell his family, "but you can contact me through my office."

When the family called the office a few days later, they were told that the worker was busy and could not come to the phone. A few days later, the family would hear the same story. And a few days later, again. And again. And forever.

The story is told of an engineer who was waiting for a bus on a Moscow street. Some men drove by and offered him a ride. He accepted. The car turned in the gates of Lubyanka Prison, and the man was never seen again.

Lubyanka Prison! A large, brownish structure just steps away from theaters, restaurants, busy streets. Here, a suspect would be searched, photographed, and fingerprinted. After his head was shaved, he would be taken to a cell. No one would tell him why he had been brought to the prison. However, he soon learned the two rules of Lubyanka. One was that he was not allowed to sleep. The other was that he must confess. Night after night, he would be dragged from his cell, pushed into a brightly lighted room, and told to confess. Stories of those scenes go like this:

"Confess to what?"
"To your disloyalty."

"What disloyalty?"

"You had better find out."

The prisoner was forbidden to sleep during the day. He was questioned throughout the night. After a few days, he would beg to know what he had done wrong. He would be given a confession to sign. With what little energy he had left, he would sign.

Many of those arrested were forced to betray fellow workers. In a typical case, a secretary would be arrested. Under torture, he would confess to crimes by both himself and his superior. Under more torture, he would implicate fellow workers.

The story was the same for farmers, factory managers, and party leaders. Concentration camps in Siberia were filling up again—with Jews whose crime was being Jewish, with former prisoners of war whose crime was not working hard enough, with factory managers whose crime was not making the workers work hard enough, with wives whose crime was not reporting on their husbands.

In March 1953, Stalin suffered a brain hemorrhage. Surprisingly, in this nation where religion had been suppressed, bearded priests of the Orthodox church were called to his bedside to pray for him.

Newspapers around the world announce the death of Stalin.

Stalin lies in state in a flower-bedecked casket. Mourning Russians, 16 abreast, formed a 10-mile line to view the body of the man who had ruled them for nearly 30 years.

He did not recover.

Svetlana wrote about her grief. "I had been a bad daughter and my father had been a bad father, but he had loved me all the same, as I loved him." Vasily attended the funeral. He was still an alcoholic and, according to Svetlana, had lost touch with reality.

For 60 hours, Stalin's body lay in state in a glass-covered, satin-lined coffin in the Lenin Mausoleum. Tens of thousands of people formed a great funeral procession, winding around Red Square, waiting for their turn to pay respects. Raw winds blew. Mourners held their coats and scarfs tight against the cold. Their breath sent columns of mist into the air.

The artillery thundered, church bells rang, and factory whistles blew in a display of respect.

Joseph Stalin, the man of steel, was dead.

/ Appendix One
Glossary

Allies During World War I, the Allies were Great Britain, France, Russia, and the United States. They fought the Central Powers—Germany, Austria-Hungary, and Turkey. During World War II, the Allies were basically the same: Great Britain, France, the Soviet Union, and the United States. They fought the Axis powers: Germany, Italy, and Japan.

Bolsheviks A communist revolutionary party advocating the overthrow of the czar. The Bolsheviks struggled against the Mensheviks for leadership.

capitalism An economic system in which business and property are owned by private companies or individuals.

cold war Term for the political tension between the Soviet Union and the United States from the end of World War II until 1989.

communism A political and economic system based on the idea that all people in a country should share wealth equally. In a communist country, all businesses and property are owned by the state.

czar An emperor.

Duma A representative body, like a parliament, under the czar.

East The term used to describe the countries that supported the Soviet Union against the United States during the cold war.

exile To force a person to leave his home, state, or country.

fascism Belief that one's nationality and race are more important than individual liberty. A Fascist supports a strong, dictatorial form of government.

Kremlin Government buildings in Moscow.

kulak A wealthy farmer.

Mensheviks A communist revolutionary party advocating overthrow of the czar. The Mensheviks struggled against the Bolsheviks for leadership.

Nazi A member of the National Socialist party that ruled Germany from 1933 to 1945 under Adolf Hitler.

NKVD The political police, who often engaged in secret activities.

purge Mass arrests and punishments to enforce loyalty.

Red Army The Bolshevik army.

ruble Money of the USSR.

secede To break away from a government.

serf A poor farmer under total control of a lord in the czar's empire.

socialism An economic system in which the government

controls most businesses and property. In Karl Marx's theory of communism, socialism is the stage a capitalistic nation must pass through before reaching true communism.

soviet   A council of Bolshevik representatives.

West   The term used to describe the countries that supported the United States against the Soviet Union during the cold war.

White Army   An army that opposed the Bolsheviks during the Russian civil war.

Appendix Two
Joseph Stalin: A
Time Line

1879—Iosif Vissarionovich Dzhugashvili (later Joseph Stalin) is born.

1894—Enrolls in a seminary.

1898—Joins a revolutionary group.

1899—Expelled from the seminary.

1900—Works with underground revolutionaries.

1901—Changes name to Koba.

1902–1924—Arrested and exiled to Siberia several times. Escapes each time.

1903—Elected a leader of the Bolsheviks (while imprisoned).

1904—Marries Ekaterina Svanidze.

1905–1908—Active in underground sabotage.

1907—Ekaterina dies, leaving one son, Yakov.

1908–1913—Arrested, imprisoned, and exiled to Siberia several times. Escapes each time.

1912—Elected to Central Committee of Bolshevik party. Edits Bolshevik newspaper, *Pravda*.

1913–1917—Remains in exile in northern Siberia.

1917—Named commissar for nationalities of new Bolshevik Soviet Republic.

1919—Elected member of Politburo; marries Nadya Alliluyev.

1922—Elected secretary general of Bolshevik party.

1922–1924—Struggles for leadership in party.

1928—Initiates First Five-Year Plan.

1929–1930—Becomes dictator of country.

1932—Nadya dies, leaving daughter, Svetlana, and son, Vasily. Initiates Second Five-Year Plan.

1933–1936—Carries out massive purges.

1936–1939   Invites journalists to attend Show Trials. Carries out massive purges.

1939—Makes pact with Hitler.

1941–1945—Faces German invasion. Joins the United States and Great Britain as an ally.

1945–1948—Establishes Soviet satellites in Eastern Europe.

1948—Imposes Berlin blockade.

1950—Opposes the United States in the Korean War.

1952—Begins new purge.

1953—Dies.

/Selected Bibliography

Readers and writers of Stalin biographies must recognize that sources abound with contradictions and misstatements. One Stalin biographer, H. Montgomery Hyde, says:

> The published literature on Stalin is enormous, since more books have been written about him than any other character in history, including Napoleon and Jesus Christ.

It is also true that Stalin ordered systematic alterations of some records and complete destruction of others. Faced with these complications, each biographer of Stalin is forced to choose those versions and explanations that seem most plausible in relationship to the other sources considered.

Below are some of the books that were used as resources for this biography.

Alliluyev, Svetlana. *Twenty Letters to a Friend.* New York: Harper & Row, 1967.

Hingley, Ronald. *Joseph Stalin, Man and Legend*. New York: McGraw-Hill, 1974.

Hyde, H. Montgomery. *Stalin, the History of a Dictator*. New York: Farrar, Straus & Giroux, 1971.

Khrushchev, Nikita. *Khrushchev Remembers*. Boston: Little, Brown, 1974.

Medvedev, Roy. *Let History Judge*. New York: Alfred A. Knopf, 1971.

Payne, Robert. *The Rise and Fall of Stalin*. New York: Simon and Schuster, 1965.

Salisbury, Harrison. *Black Night, White Snow*. New York: G. P. Putnam's Sons, 1953.

Svanidze, Budu. *My Uncle Joseph Stalin*. New York: G. P. Putnam's Sons, 1953.

Ulam, Adam. *Stalin, the Man and His Era*. New York: Viking Press, 1973.

Volkogonov, Dmitri. *Stalin, Triumph and Tragedy*. New York: Grove Weidenfeld, 1991.

Index